MW01700498

Who Is

Wearing The Pants?

Live Healthier, Happier, and Richer!

By David R. Hearld

To ~~Pat~~

Thanks for your inspiration and being a great example of "Wearing the Pants?" You are one of the best "Big Pic" (BS 53) I have ever met!

Sept 2010

Introduction

Who Is Wearing The Pants? is a versatile resource that inspires you to take control of your life by reducing stress, managing anger, staying motivated, and being happy in everyday life. It instills hope and strength even in the darkest of places, where many of us find ourselves during times of economic uncertainty, sickness, or family crisis.

This book consists of 15 short, precise and easy-to-read Mini-Books under one cover. Printed on the back are The Pant Principles discussed in each Mini-Book, which will enhance specific areas of your life that you think may need improvement.

These Mini-Books take less time to read than a restaurant menu and there is something for everyone to learn, whether you are the boss, head of household, a senior citizen, teenager, or new entry-level employee.

Who Is Wearing The Pants? is a "Leadership Book." By applying the Pant Principles others will admire and respect you and offer the gifts of friendship, love, and even business opportunities, even if you are a leader of only one – YOU.

This is a motivational "Get Ready" instructional guide to help you accomplish any goal or dream. All of those diet, workout, and how to fix-it/build-it books are useless until you are truly ready to start and stick to the process.

Who Is Wearing The Pants? is a "Health Book" for your mind, body, and soul. By following The Pant Principles you will live longer, healthier, happier, and richer.

This is a "Sales Book" to teach how to improve and enhance the value of YOU – and how to influence others to listen and to want to accept your ideas and values.

This teaching guide is motivational for people of all ages and backgrounds, interlaced with entertainment, humor, and my personal stories and experiences. Through practical techniques encompassing the study of Organizational Behavior that can be applied to relationships with family, friends, and business associates, this workbook has the power to help you command higher levels of respect and success in every aspect of your life.

Who Is Wearing The Pants? will help you a little, or it can help a lot. To get the most from this book, start at the beginning and read each Mini-Book in order. Think about how you can apply these principles to your life before moving on to the next chapter.

Unlike many books that simply tell you what to do, you will soon learn to practice The Pant Principles that will teach you to reach the levels of respect, self-control, and happiness you desire – making you a doer, *not* just a dreamer.

Enjoy!

David

Reviews:

"I have just finished reading and re-reading every line of your great book, Who Is Wearing The Pants? What a joy! Every chapter was motivational and fun to read. I found the "Break Free" section especially useful in teaching how to break bad habits. Most of us go through life developing more and more bad habits without a clue of how to get rid of them. You have found a quick and easy method for everyone to find that magic moment when they are able to, as you say, "Break Free." I will be looking forward to your next book!"

Vin Haggan – Composer, songwriter, and author of "Haggan Notes."

"This was one of the best books I have ever read about personal development and leadership skills, and is a must-read for anyone wanting to improve their position in life. Who Is Wearing The Pants? has something for everyone because it targets 15 behavior patterns that effect how others evaluate us and how we believe we really are.

If you're seeking to move up a level by way of promotion, making more money, or dreaming big about owning your own business, this is a book for you. If you want to be admired by others, this is a book for you. And if you are 100% happy with who you are, this is a book for you too, so you can understand the strengths and challenges others are facing. Understanding people better is the first step to helping others. Understanding yourself is a must to reach your fullest potential.

I found the book down to earth with a solid level of realism; I enjoyed reading every page of this inspiring and motivational masterpiece."

John Amico – Founder of John Amico Hair Care Products, Chairman of Share the Wealth Salon System, franchise and business consultant, former franchiser and national business speaker

"An exquisite gem of a book that takes you in several different directions to improve your quality of life. I particularly enjoyed the chapter on making money and retaining integrity at the same time. The ideas are presented in a simple yet eloquent manner. Once you start reading the book you will find it hard to put down."

Dr. Denise Wood -- M.A.,Psychology.D. Coauthor of "Secrets Why He Wants to Cheat/Secrets Why She Wants to Cheat."

"Dave Hearld has hit a home run with his book about gaining self-respect and staying in control. By the end of the book, another leader is born, and it could be you. It's a great read for both genders of all ages, and should stay on the publisher's best selling book list for years!"

Richard Valentine – Published Author

"After I read your book I went out and bought three pairs of new shoes. I had been delaying and had a favorite pair of black flats – after reading the chapter, Happy Souls, I knew it was time. I also recommended your book to my Easter Seals CEO group."

Lynn Sinnott – President/CEO Easter Seals Volusia, Flagler, Florida

"This is the best book I have ever read. When I bought it I thought it was only about learning about leadership and to get respect, but I have learned so much more. Thanks to your chapter, Keep Your Pants On, I am doing better at work and with my family, and I rarely get mad anymore, especially at other drivers. After reading your book three times, I've learned something new each time. It is incredible!"

Danny Smith – Construction Forman, Los Angeles, California

"Who Is Wearing The Pants? is a thought-provoking, common-sense approach to solving one of life's most wanted desires: RESPECT. While the title immediately grabbed my attention, it soon became apparent that this is one of those books you don't put down. Each chapter has numerous descriptions of everyday situations that, depending on how handled, can bring or lose respect. The bonus is, this book is very motivational and has helped me to break bad habits and to get things accomplished.

This book reminds us that RESPECT is never given, but earned through deliberate actions of the individual. This book should be carried along as a quick refresher, and an affirmation technique to use on a daily basis. It is a book that you can keep for immediate inspiration to remind and to learn one of life's simple but basic secrets. It is a book that should be read by students, businesspeople, salespeople, parents, and everyone who has ever asked, 'Why don't they respect me?'

This is a book that will stand along with my all-time favorites like: How to Win Friends and Influence People, One Minute Manager, and I'm OK, You're OK. I see Who Is Wearing The Pants? as a great gift to give others to share and motivate in a powerful, yet basic way. I plan to give this book to friends, business associates, and even my kids."

Ken Galt – Landscape Architect, Chicago, Illinois

"This is a wonderful book. I just finished reading it and did not put it down until I was done. This was great. Well written. I am going to use your teachings every day. A while back, an old friend told me that I was stupid. I felt discouraged and I believed she was right. I loved your chapter, Stay In Your Garden. After reading this, I feel good about me, and I now know how to stay in control of myself. Thank you for your inspiration! Congratulations again for an outstanding piece of work."

Lucy Perajica – Workaholic and first-generation Croatian

"I grew up in the era when men ruled and we women were subservient. In your story, you didn't differentiate and that, of course, was encouraging to me. I have always felt insecure and yet have always tried to hide it. I loved the chapter Forgive Your Past, and I'm working on doing that. You have inspired me to hold my head up high, believe in myself, and know that I'm okay. To inspire others is a great accomplishment."

Carol Farran – Mother of two girls, Midwest, USA

"Yikes! After reading David Hearld's book I realized I've been shimmying into work with my pants down around my ankles. As a college math professor, I'm great in the classroom but lost in office politics. Didn't take long before a "snake in the grass," as Dave says, got me. Following Dave's Pant Principles I'll know what to do next time.

I now proudly and confidently go to work, shoes shined, and my pants firmly belted around my waist. Thanks, Dave!"

John Sinnott – Professor of Mathematics, Daytona State College, Florida

I loved reading, "Who Is Wearing The Pants?" While reading, I was reminded of my past "Career Days" and it was nice to be re-inspired again. I used each chapter (or should I say each pair of pants) as a tool to personally improve my life today, not only for myself but all those I come in contact with. Thanks again for the inspiration."

Suzi Hood – Loving life while living with MS

Ten percent of the proceeds from the sale of
<u>Who Is Wearing The Pants?</u>
is equally donated to the following Organizations.

Cancer and Mental Health Research.

Who Is

Wearing The Pants?

Live Healthier, Happier, and Richer!

By David R. Hearld

Published by: **Gibraltar Group, Inc.**

Distributed by: **Profit-Tell International, Inc.**

201 E. Ogden Ave, Suite 112
Hinsdale, IL 60521
Phone: 630-655-3700
Fax: 630-655-4100
Email: Sales@Profit-Tell.com

Who Is Wearing The Pants?

Website: *www.WhoIsWearingThePants.com*

Email: *PantSecrets@aol.com*

For corporate inquiries for bulk purchase discounts call:
Toll free 1- 877-78- Pants (1- 877-787-2687)

Brand Copyright © 2008

First Edition - 2009

Copy Editor: Laura Bliss Plekavic

Book Cover Design by: Tim Rohlwing

by Gibraltar Group Publishing

All rights reserved. No part of this book shall be reproduced or transmitted in any form by any magnetic, electronic or mechanical means including photocopying, or recording, without proper written permission from the publisher. No patent or copyright liability is assumed with respect to the content, nor liability assumed for damages resulting from the use of the information contained herein.

ISBN: 978-0-9822740-0-2

Follow The Process

Pant Check Three

Pant Check Four

Pant Check Five

Pant Check Finale

The Process

Solving the Mystery of Respect

"Wearing the pants" is an old adage that originated centuries ago, referring to the dominant role men held in the household. Quite literally, it developed as a representation of male authority, as males were the only gender "allowed" to wear pants. Today, the idiom "wearing the pants" has come to describe a person of either gender, wearing a skirt, shorts, or nothing at all, *who is in control in any situation*, family, school or group, *but especially in control of himself or herself.*

Respect: it is the most essential characteristic of wearing the pants and is the essential aspect of *being in control of yourself.* Some people gain plenty of respect, but you would be surprised at how many possess absolutely none. Most of us are somewhere right in the middle, and *all* of us want more.

Pant Secret

Respect – Can't buy it, but some have it because they are rich and beautiful. Can't demand it, but some have it because they are in a position of power. But there is one surefire way to get more respect – by *earning* it!

On the surface that sounds easy, but you will come to find out earning respect is actually a *learned* skill that requires effort and plenty of practice. In this book, I will refer to wearing the pants as a component of the magical formula to aid you in earning and holding respect.

Many of us *may not want to be a leader or dramatically change our lives.* But most of us want to *enhance* our lives ... maybe by striving to lose weight, getting things done, being treated better by those we love or people we work with, feeling better about ourselves, gaining control of our emotions, being calm and happy, or maybe making more money. Small life adjustments such as these have been scientifically linked to better health. According to a study in *Proceedings of the National Academy of Sciences*, the happiest participants had lower levels of the stress hormone cortisol, *and* lower increases of plasma fibrinogen, a sign of inflammation that can predict heart disease.

The easiest way to enhance your life is to gain, retain, and give respect!

Pant Secret

Hard work may provide some self-respect, *but in itself does not generate respect from others.* We all know of someone who brings his or her laptop on vacation ... spends their Saturday nights at the office ... or forgets numerous family celebrations. You know ... the ones who live to work, not work to live ... but does all their work pay off? Do these over-achievers truly get the respect they deserve? In many cases, probably not! This may be you.

Getting respect can be as grand and thrilling as the physical act of disappearance, or something as subtle as a sleight of hand trick. We see magic performed right in front of us, yet we can't unravel its secret. Magicians fascinate us with their skill and the illusions they have honed through years of practice and learning. But is it *really* "magic"?

We've all heard someone claim that their boss, professor or coach *"demanded respect."* But this phrase has become so overused, its become an oxymoron. Just as the world wasn't created in a single day, the ability to obtain respect does not emerge overnight. You're not born with it, and you certainly cannot demand to be respected. Leaders are not born with a pre-determined genetic code that establishes them as such; they are instead made leaders through extensive training, education, mentoring, experience, and the pursuit of self-development in earning the respect needed to successfully lead.

When this occurs, leaders then *command* respect, and their behavior *naturally causes* a respectful response from others. In a relatively short amount of time, you can change the way you are perceived by your existing circle, and then extend outward to reach other people of influence – just by becoming a little more self-aware! Over the last 30 years I have conducted extensive research through observing, studying and teaching, to discover 15 fundamental personality characteristics that help develop respect. I have dubbed these patterns:

"The Pant Principles"

I have learned from countless respected leaders who have shared their success stories about how they achieved and maintained their respect and power. Vice versa, I have also discovered that a cloud of disrespect hanging over you or those in your circle can cause loss of income, opportunity for advancement, or popularity with your peers. The Pant Principles I have developed will teach how to change this negativity.

I should clarify that I am not a psychologist, nor do I claim to be an expert in the field of human behavior; rather, I am a businessman and entrepreneur who has gained a wealth of knowledge at the street level by researching and familiarizing myself with the positive and negative results relating to human behavior.

It is through these experiences that I have developed methods for teaching individuals to improve their positive behavior, eliminate the negative, and earn respect. After all, isn't respect one of the greatest hallmarks of success? I have taught these principles to hundreds of associates and have been fueled by their positive responses. This has inspired me to pass along my secrets and lead you on a journey of gaining respect that is easy, fun and magical.

Just like the magician and his tricks, leaders have discovered the secrets behind gaining the respect to elevate their presence and grant them the self-confidence needed to captivate an audience, even if the audience consists of a single follower. This is the "magical" formula I will share with you.

Who Is Wearing the Pants? is for people of any age and background who want to command a higher level of respect and success. Whether you are the boss, a new entry-level employee, the head of household, a senior citizen, or a teenager faced with the challenges of adolescence, the following insights will help unlock the mystery of respect.

This is also a powerful instructional tool offering practical techniques to apply to relationships with family, friends and business associates. This is a "Get Ready" guide to help you level the playing field ... and help you rise above to be *motivated to finish what you start.*

Pant Secret

Do you own or manage a business? As a form of "Organizational Behavior," apply these principles to employees, vendors and customers, and you will experience great rewards in the form of reduced employee turnover, lower costs, higher sales, enhanced customer loyalty, and increased financial success.

And best of all ... *peace of mind!*

The Pant Principles: The Process

Forgive Your Past (p. 15): Live in the present and *feel good about yourself, boost self-respect, and live happier.*

Create Your Future (p. 22): Build your self-esteem and make better decisions to *improve your life.*

Use Self-Control (p. 27): Always *be in control* and *live longer* by managing your emotions.

Learn Meditation Techniques (p. 33): Learn how to always *feel safe and secure.*

Look Like a Winner (p. 40): Simple secrets to *looking and feeling* like a million bucks.

Ditch Bad Habits (p. 45): Rid yourself of embarrassing habits in a snap – literally! *Live healthier.*

Be Likeable (p. 51): Feel good about yourself – win friends and influence people without being overbearing.

Learn Self-Defense (p. 60): How to *protect yourself* with assertion – not aggression.

Control Adversaries (p. 67): Don't let your enemies "rattle" you. *Stay in control* so you won't get caught with your pants down.

Develop Courage (p. 73): Learn how to stand up for yourself and those close to you *without fear.*

Manage Time Effectively (p. 81): Save time and *increase your perceived value* by becoming "invisible." *Live richer.*

Become Persuasive (p. 89): How to get what you want … negotiate *so everyone wins.*

Become a Mentor (p. 98): Feel great about inspiring someone to succeed and improve their life.

Reach Goals (p. 107): Follow a plan to help you *reach your goals and dreams.*

Have Commitment (p. 113): Feel good about becoming a *doer*, not just a *dreamer.*

Many of you may already be practicing some of these Pant Principles and perhaps this book will enhance your techniques. Others may choose to select a few to improve specific aspects of their lives. And if you need a complete respect makeover, every page of this book is for you.

Pant Secret

When you start wearing the pants in every walk of life, you will *feel a change in your personal power.* An added bonus? The tips and secrets to effective respect-building are *short, sweet, and easy to remember!*

The world is full of people telling us WHAT we should do. But rarely does anyone show us HOW to do it.

Unlike many guides that simply tell you what to do, you will soon learn and begin to practice the Pant Principles to *guide, teach, and motivate you how* to reach whatever level of respect you desire.

"Get Ready" to change at least one thing about your life.

Focus on the process and let your journey begin!

Note: This is also a workbook. You will see fill-in-the-blank areas *(Pant Lessons)* in several of the chapters. Do not speed-read past these opportunities to apply the Pant Principles to your life. Take the time to fill them in with your specifics; it will only *benefit you!* There is no rush on this journey, so sit back and enjoy the ride.

Pant Check One

Building Self-Respect

Before you read the next section, please indicate how you feel about your level of Self-Respect at/in:

	LOW				HIGH
Home:	**0**	**1**	**2**	**3**	**4**
Work:	**0**	**1**	**2**	**3**	**4**
Social settings:	**0**	**1**	**2**	**3**	**4**

Today's Date: ______________________________

Throw Away
Those Old Bell-Bottoms

Pant Principle – Forgive Your Past

Required Attire – New, Clean Pants
(New Bell-Bottoms Are Okay Too!)

It's impossible to respect someone who doesn't respect themselves.

Earning and gaining respect must begin with *allowing yourself to be respected.* Memories, both good and bad, are an integral part of our lives and shape who we are today. Some use good memories to stay "safely" locked in the past. Others dwell on bad memories, hindering the ability to grow and accept a new path.

Think of your past as a wardrobe of memories. All of us have a few items in our mental closets that need to be discarded. And if you literally have a wardrobe filled with polyester suits, platform shoes, bell-bottoms, and flowered shirts saying "peace, love and happiness," it's probably a good indication you are guilty of living in the past. Let's begin the path to earning respect on the right foot by getting rid of our tired old wardrobe and replacing it with a fresh outlook on life.

"On no account brood over your wrong-doing. Rolling in the muck is not the best way of getting clean."

~ Aldous Huxley (1894 - 1963) ~

Our personal histories tell stories of heartbreak, grievances, or failures. Perhaps you've experienced a divorce, suffered wounds inflicted by war, been fired from a job, or mourned the death of a loved one. How long will you feel sorry for yourself, be angry, disappointed, or hurt? A day, a year, or the rest of your life? In order to earn respect, you must have self-respect. The first step to respecting yourself is accepting your past and using it to move forward.

The past we are discussing could have happened last year, last week, or yesterday. Maybe you were in a minor traffic accident, had a root canal, or your stock portfolio took a hit. It is something negative that is affecting how you live today. Use these same principles to move on.

Pant Secret

The speed with which you put on a fresh new pair of pants and confront your feelings of guilt, anger and despair determines your future and *how others respect you.* You may never forget your misfortune, but you will learn to come to terms with it. Remembering how strong you became and the pride you felt in overcoming the event will leave you with an inner peace far outweighing the pain and negative emotions.

The mind is an incredible instrument, a computer programmed to create mighty warriors, gifted scholars and vicious felons. The brain in your head *is yours to command – not the reverse.* As you control your mind, you control everything: your body, your emotions, your outcome in life, and your *self-respect*.

If you had the chance, would you change your history? Of course, there are past events I would like to change, but it is not possible. Even the most insignificant change would alter who I am today. I like the pants I' am wearing, but it wasn't always so.

Pant Parable

When I was 14, my family experienced a horrific tragedy with the loss of my older sister in a fatal automobile accident caused by a drunk driver. This was a life-altering event for everyone in my family circle. It was easy to become resentful when we would witness a reckless driver. With time, I came to understand there was nothing I could do about controlling other drivers, but I realized I could change my own behavior by mastering awareness of my position on the road, keeping distance, and staying alert. My sister's death is truly an event we will never forget, but one keeping me out of accidents and saving my family from danger on many occasions.

Pant Secret

Learn something positive from every bad event. It is nearly impossible to move on from past mistakes until a positive memory replaces the unpleasant one. This will allow your brain to detach negative emotions from the memory and keep it in your past where it belongs.

Do you know those who have consistently made bad decisions? Perhaps such "bad" decisions were made based on instant gratification: *"I've just got to have that gorgeous new designer dress."* Or perhaps laziness: *"This 10-year-old pair of jeans is fine for the interview. They'll never notice."*

Consider those who fit the above description: those who shrug-off mistakes with, *"I really screwed that up. Oh well, I'm not perfect!"* And there are those who use the excuse, "I'm not as smart/cute/good/quick as ... so I can't do as well as ...!" Do you have a high level of respect for this kind of nonchalant attitude? Self-respect is gained by solving and correcting your mistakes. Think to yourself, "I could have made a better decision, and I will be smarter next time!"

If you are a bona fide dweller of the "bad stuff" in your past, then learn to dwell on the "good stuff." Replace bad memories with recollections of good feelings: the race you won, a certificate of achievement, a promotion, gratitude from someone you helped, or volunteering for community service. When you think of those accomplishments, recall the great feelings of pride and the self-respect you earned.

Pant Secret

Build on the good stuff. It's just as easy to think about good things as it is bad things, but healthier, and more fun!

Think back and recall the BEST memory from your past. Write it down: ______________________________

____

____

Those who LEARN from their past without LIVING in it, earn respect.

Being *emotionally* attached to good memories can also shape your present and future. We are surrounded by people who cannot or do not want to let go of the past. *"Hey, there's "football" Eddie! Wasn't he voted 'Most Likely to Name His First Child after the High School Mascot'?"* And yes, there is 57-year-old Eddie with his senior jacket, and he hasn't changed one bit, still thinking he *demands* respect.

In life, if you expect a free handout, chances are you will be in an incredibly long line with a forever wait.

Pant Secret

Some choose to be victims of past circumstance, as they enjoy being pitied or the center of attention. Perhaps they even think the world owes them something. Are you emotionally stuck in the past, still wearing those old bell-bottom pants? Do you really want to be remembered as "the person who never grew up?"

"Yesterday is history.

Tomorrow is a mystery.

And today? Today is a gift.

That's why we call it the present."

~Babatunde Olatunji (1927 - 2003) ~

Pant Parable

When I was 12 years old, I was trying to impress a pretty girl in my class. I had long, gangly legs and decided to jump over a fire hydrant, thinking I would impress her with my "incredible" athletic abilities. Then disaster struck! My jump was not high enough and with my legs straddling the iron monster, I heard the terrible sound of my pants being snagged in the most embarrassing place imaginable. Worse yet, I happened to be wearing my favorite purple (yes, purple) corduroy pants.

For the next 20 years, I thought about my embarrassing attempt to impress Sarah. I never had the courage to let her know how I felt about her after my embarrassing stunt with the fire hydrant. Later at our high school reunion, she and I talked about the fun we had together back in the day. I reminded her of the pants ordeal and guess what she said ... "Oh, really? I don't remember that at all. I always thought you were cute, but you never acted as if you liked me!"

At that moment, I threw those old corduroys out of my mental closet along with the negative memory, replacing it with a positive one ... she thought I was cute! I finally forgave myself and turned my self-imposed embarrassment into a funny memory. Of course despite our best efforts, it's sometimes hard to forget or forgive those split corduroys and put them behind us.

What things do you have stored in your closet? Use all the energy you're wasting with "what-if" and "if-only" and put it into building a better, more positive future. Write ONE memory down and decide to take it out of your closet, and throw it away.

A negative memory I WILL remove from my closet is:

____

I'm able to let go of this mental baggage because I learned

______________________________ from this experience.

When you throw away the negativity, choose *another* to remove from your closet.

Pant Secret

> You may always have the scar, but you'll forget the pain causing it.

Let go of regrets, anger, or frustration as you would let go of a really ugly yearbook picture. Yes, it's a fact you looked like that once, but you don't anymore. The reins of life are held tightly in your grasp – take the opportunity to guide your own destiny. Once you've accepted your past, you've shown you can *respect yourself* and others will do the same! BE FREE – LET GO (of those old bell-bottoms pants)!

The past cannot be who you are, but who you were. Today is who you are. And tomorrow is who you WANT to be.

Today is Tomorrow's Past

Pant Principle – Create Your Future

(While you are at it, change your past, too!)

Required Attire – Slip-On Pants

Take a look at your watch and note the time.

The last chapter discussed letting go of bad memories and explored the notion that our personal histories, past decisions, and circumstances help to establish who we are today.

Ever heard the saying, "Why do bad things happen to good people?" The truth is that we *all* go through life with little power to control many of the things that happen to us. *It's the manner in which we handle these situations that grants us control over our destinies,* instead of letting fate do it for us. This chapter is about *choice* and about learning to make decisions in order to *create* the kind of future we want.

Pant Secret

Here we are today, wanting and needing more respect and recognition from our peers. The road to earning respect is *directly controlled by the decisions we make that will influence our life and the lives of those around us.*

The next time you hear your conscience whispering in your ear, *"This might be a mistake; this can't be good for me,"* don't complain about the aftermath if you yield to temptation.

A particular decision may or may not have been worth the risk; you made the choice and it became your past. It was your choice to wear tiger-striped bell-bottom pants to the formal dinner; so accept the stares, glares, and laughter, and step over it to move on. Next time you'll have *learned from your mistakes,* and most likely make a more appropriate decision.

Now look at your watch again.

Do you realize you just changed your past? Thirty seconds ago, you decided to continue reading this chapter. You could have watched TV, had a donut, gossiped with a friend, or taken a nap but instead you read on.

What kind of past do you want? How would you like to be remembered?

Pant Lesson:

I would like my business associates to remember me for:

____

I would like my family to remember me for:

____

I would like my friends to remember me for:

____

Pant Secret

CARPE DIEM! – "Seize the Day"
Or, someone will take it from you.

Become more aware that every action (or lack thereof) affects your past. Everything you do, say, think, or feel instantaneously becomes your yesterday.

Changing your past is truly as easy as slipping on another pair of pants. Do the right thing today and everything else will fall into line. Create your future by adhering to the following:

The Building Blocks of Self-Respect

Be accountable

Do what you say you're going to do and always be on time. Being late is disrespectful to others and to *YOURSELF!*

Work towards achieving your goals

If you want an orderly office or home in the future, put things away when you're done.

If you want a healthy bank account and smaller waistline, choose water over that mocha latté half-caff with whipped cream.

If you want a healthy body, choose to use the stairs instead of opting for the elevator.

If you want to meet more people, project a friendly attitude. Make eye contact and smile no matter how you may feel at the time.

Be responsible for *your* actions

You are NOT invisible. People are watching and remembering what you do and how you act. Unless you have entered a drinking contest, you're not going to earn respect if you're caught slamming shots of tequila at the local bar. Oh, and if you are in a drinking contest – *WIN, but never complain about the hangover.*

Pant Secret

> When my goals and tasks seem unmanageable and I think to myself, "How in the world am I going to accomplish all of this?," then I *start one step at a time,* and before I know, it's done.

Pant Lesson: *Get it Done*

Right now, choose one small project left undone at your residence: let's say painting a door. Turn off the TV and take one step toward the paint can in the garage. As you take the first step the other foot will follow and before you know it, the door is finished. *Every time* you open the door, you will feel gratified and you will continue to fuel your *self-esteem.*

Think about putting on a pair of pants, one leg at a time. The answer to handling a huge to-do list, a pile of laundry, a cluttered garage, or even starting a business is to accomplish one thing at a time. When tomorrow arrives, today becomes yesterday and will be a good day in your past.

Another key ingredient in building self-respect? Think positively! You have heard this before and now is time to live it.

Do you view the proverbial glass as half-empty or half-full? Everything in life is a choice: it's up to *you* to look for the silver lining. Numerous studies have found that optimism not only helps people get more enjoyment out of life, but it also helps prevent illness, preserve emotional health, and increase longevity. It's all a matter of perception. Make the commitment to view negative experiences as growing opportunities and your glass will continue to fill.

What does this have to do with wearing the pants, and earning respect?

Simple! When you are recognized as a doer and when you adopt a positive mentality, people will flock to you, admire you, and give you respect. They will like your style and fancy your fashion. You will become known for your good decisions.

You will build trust by ensuring the decisions you make are good ones. Other "pant-wearers" will seek your advice and choose to be seen in your company.

It's all about 30 seconds.

Take that extra time to *change* your past and *determine* your future. The choice you make now influences what happens in the next 30 seconds.

"Yesterday is gone.
Tomorrow has not yet come.
We have only today.
Let us begin."

~ Mother Teresa (1910-1997) ~

Keep Your Pants On

Pant Principle – Use Self-Control

Required Attire – Lightweight Pants with a Good Belt

So you have your new pants on ... but how well do they fit? How easy are they to keep on? Just because you've tried them for size does *not* mean you are *wearing the pants.* They may not fit well in the beginning. It takes time and experience to learn how to wear them properly, to adapt to you, and your style.

You've heard the phrase, *"Hey, keep your pants on!"* referring to someone being impatient or showing anger. *"Just calm down already!" "Cool your jets!"*

Pant Secret

When you are wearing the pants to gain control of your life and earn respect, you must always remain levelheaded and *STAY IN CONTROL!* Otherwise, you are certain to lose respect – and your pants too. Being levelheaded means being aware of yourself, your actions, and your emotions and learning to keep them under control. It means communicating displeasure without showing anger and being able to modify unacceptable behavior without a battle. By staying cool under the toughest of pressure, you're not only showing you're the stronger person but are instantly building self-respect as well as respect from others.

Earning respect is a lifelong endeavor and grows one step at a time. On the other hand, *losing* respect can happen in just a few seconds. Losing your temper and yelling at someone, or blaring your horn and screaming obscenities will *instantly* expunge any existing levels of respect. As the saying goes ... control your emotions; don't let them control *you*. This will give you strength of character.

Wearing the pants means acting like a traffic cop, directing all of your actions, thoughts, and energy into positive channels. There is no room in your pants for negative energy. Like the fumes from a filthy exhaust, negative energy permeates the atmosphere, creeping into every aspect of our lives and making our pants reek.

If stress from these negative energies is becoming persistent and you're finding it hard to control, it's time do something about it. Important research from the British Medical Journal finds that stress is linked to the development of heart disease, type 2 diabetes, and other health-damaging behaviors such as heavy drinking, smoking, and lack of exercise.

Wearing the pants means using *self-discipline* to control unwanted stress, anger, fears, and any uncertainty affecting your attitude, mind, health, and spirit. It means focusing on your emotions and being aware of how you feel ... almost like becoming a self-therapist. It is healthy and natural to feel and be aware of negative emotions. *The key to wearing the pants is "keeping your pants on" – learning how to transform negative emotions into positive behavior to generate personal power and respect.* This is the first step in improving self-discipline.

Pant Secret

Our emotions are active and alive 24 hours a day ... even in our dreams. For many, it's much too easy to allow these emotions to control our lives and the important relationships within them ... but *not if you are wearing the pants!*

All emotions can be divided into three areas: *good, neutral, and bad.* This chapter will focus primarily on "keeping your pants on" when confronted with the "bad" emotions, like anger, envy, disappointment, jealousy, frustration, etc. At times, it may seem downright impossible to control your emotions. How do you react when your spouse lets you down? Your child misbehaves? Your employee, co-worker, or employer disrespects you? Did you let anger control your thoughts and actions?

Was your head swarming with negative emotions that triggered an unhealthy response? Were you able to keep your pants on? Probably not! And most likely you lost respect because of your reaction in just those few seconds.

I have studied countless methods of anger management, for during my adolescent years, my temper was something ferocious and often out of control. *Recognizing that I had a problem was the first and hardest step toward overcoming the roadblock to "keeping my pants on" and earning respect.*

Pant Parable

My father was the calmest person I have ever known. I never saw him angry and he always stayed in control. When a negative situation occurred and a family member would complain or get angry, he would say, "Oh, what about it!" But the way he said it, was magical. His voice would start at a high pitch and end at a low pitch and sounded like, "Eeeeeww wut abow it." The funny way he said it made everyone laugh and quickly diminished the drama created by the circumstance. It was impossible to stay angry for long. I still practice this every day. Go ahead, try to say it ... my dad would be proud and happy if you use it!

Pant Secret

Even though we may be powerless over the emotions we *feel*, we hold the power to control the responses resulting from these emotions and therefore, the power to control our own destinies.

We can also learn how to *avoid or diffuse* situations during which negative emotions emerge, preventing these feelings from taking control of our minds. Becoming the master of your emotions – keeping your pants on in any situation – means constantly monitoring what you are feeling: good *or* bad. For the sake of this chapter, let us focus on how your body reacts to negative emotions. Does your stomach clench when faced with a threat? Do your shoulders stiffen when someone approaches? Does your face flush or do you break out in a sweat when you are put in an unpleasant situation?

What caused you to feel this way? How can you change it, and how can you avoid that feeling again? Once you acknowledge these negative emotions as they begin to take control, you must immediately remove yourself from the situation, or better yet:

Learn to respond before you react!

There are many times in order *for you to keep your pants on, you will need to permit others to keep theirs on, too!* The best scenario to discuss a problem, or disagreement, is for *everyone* to remain cool, calm, *and in control.*

To wear the pants, there is one phrase to *NEVER* allow to escape from your mouth, and it usually starts with the word, YOU.

"You did this and ...," or "It's all your fault ...."

If you utter these forbidden phrases, you have *lost control* of the conversation, as the opponent will go into self-defense mode and *lose their calm and pants* at the same time. The Pant Response is to say, *"You may be right,* but this is how I feel about ...." "You may be right" is one of my favorite methods for keeping a situation calm, and everyone keeps their self-respect.

Pant Parable

Recently, I was waiting for a table in an upscale restaurant and noticed four tables needing to be bussed. After 10 minutes of waiting and seeing no one in the process of the cleanup, I asked the host, "Do you know how long it will take for our table to be ready?" I was informed, "Everyone is on break and it will be a bit longer before you can be seated." Feeling my blood pressure rising, I was nearing the edge of anger. I winked at her and replied, "That's okay, you need more help and I'm your guy!"

I walked over to the nearest table and proceeded to remove the dirty dinnerware onto the nearby cart. I smiled at the waiter and let him know, "We have been waiting on a table, the wait staff was on break, and I simply wanted to help." Normally waiters do not clean tables, but this one sure did! He and I had the table cleaned in less than one minute.

Actually, it was quite fun! Instead of allowing myself to feel negative emotions, I stayed calm and kept my pants on (and allowed them to keep theirs on) – a proactive approach that turned the situation into an evening of positive memories.

Pant Secret

Keeping your pants on does not mean you must never appear to be irritated or angry. Unfortunately, you'll find many people do not respond to calmness. Leaders *do* raise their voice or give "the look" *when appropriate*. The illusion this emits is quite powerful: a calm, cool persona contrasted by an outward display of displeasure through the power of body language, actions, and tone of voice. A good presenter has mastered this trick as he or she yells and appears to be upset, while in reality, is focusing on the "act" of being angry to motivate listeners by using emotions.

Learning to wear the pants may not always be easy – they're going to get snagged and dirtied but a little care and repair work will get them back into shape. Lightweight Pants are "one size fits all." The rules and principles are the same for everyone. All you have to do is shift your habits and thought processes by converting bad emotions into good ones. Suddenly, the pants begin to fit, and so does *self-respect*.

***"If you would cure anger, do not feed it.
Say to yourself,
'I used to be angry every day,'
then every other day,
now only every third or fourth day.
When you reach thirty days
be thankful."***

~Epictetus (55 - 135AD) ~

Okay, David – All of this sounds great, but how do you control your emotions? I have tried and tried, and it's just not that easy!

Stay in Your Garden

Pant Principle – Learn Meditation Techniques

Required Attire – Comfortable Leisure Pants

As we have discussed, respect can be lost in the blink of an eye – much more quickly than it can be gained. Before we move on to earning respect, it is critically important to learn the virtue of self-control, an essential ingredient in building self-respect.

There are 1000s of methods and many books devoted to the topic of meditation and biofeedback. If you have not developed your own techniques for *keeping your pants on,* let me share with you a simple process I use to serve as a guide to controlling emotions.

Pant Secret

You may be aware of Qigong (pronounced chee gong), which literally translates as "energy skill." Qigong is an ancient Chinese self-healing practice, similar to tai chi, that works through the use of unique breathing patterns, various physical postures, and motions of the hands and arms. *It teaches you to focus intensely on good thoughts, good memories, and pleasant sensations.* A main objective of this practice is to create a safe, warm, friendly place – a mental garden – in which you can relax and regenerate your mind and spirit.

You too can create your own mental garden: a place to go when you wish to stay in control. *Only good feelings are permitted in your garden.*

Neutral feelings are only allowed at the outer edge, and negative feelings are banned entirely. Complaints, jealousy, rudeness, bullies, tailgaters ... any and all bad situations or negative influences are forbidden from entering your garden.

In life, unpleasant situations are inevitable. However, by keeping your pants on – maintaining your position in your garden – you can keep these feelings safely at bay. Should you allow negativity from others to affect you, you are leaving your garden and thereby entering their emotional territory. Practice staying positive in every situation you encounter and it will become a good habit.

Sadness and grief are also emotions that can invade our lives. Sometimes these emotions present themselves suddenly, and other times we have a chance to prepare for the grief that lies ahead. Keeping your pants on in such situations is possible as well. Return to your garden and with practice, you will gradually be able to reduce healing time and focus on the positive memories that you will carry with you for a lifetime.

Pant Secret

Focus on the positives and your garden will flourish. Negative thoughts are the weeds, with no place inside your garden. If you let them cultivate and run wild, they will eventually take over and destroy the good, including self-respect.

Focusing on the positive does NOT mean becoming a recluse and isolating yourself from negativity. Instead, it is a way to put up a "force shield" to protect your self-esteem from the negative energy of people who want to rock your boat.

It does not mean you can ignore your responsibilities or avoid dealing with adverse situations. Going to your garden simply puts you into the proper frame of mind to handle just about anything that comes your way.

Your garden is the only place to *store all of your precious memories and accomplishments.* Just like a bank vault protecting your valuable assets, no one has the combination except you.

Pant Secret

The next time an aggressive driver cuts you off or *flips* you off, and you want to roll down the window and get your revenge, use this Pant Secret until you have it mastered.

Look at the other driver who has lost their pants with a surprised look, point at them and act like they are a long-lost friend and say, "Oh, I know you!" Smile and wave with enthusiasm. That gets them every time, and you stay in control!

Tip: Keep your window up and you will not hear their negativity.

Pant Secret

People who wear the pants do not avoid negative situations. By remaining calm on the inside, they are better able to make logical, effective decisions deduced from conscious thought. Leaders make *rational* – NOT emotional or reactive – decisions. *Only* make decisions while you are *inside* of your garden where you are safe and sound.

Whenever I find myself in a negative situation, all I say to myself is, "Boy, I'm way out of my garden; I need to get back." Saying those words helps me get out of an emotional space and into a rational one that focuses on the issue at hand. If someone says that phrase to you, "Hey, keep your pants on!" it's time for you to scamper back to your garden, where *you're in control.*

Okay – let's do it!

Let's create your safe space, the place of happy feelings and memories ... your perfect garden.

Pant Secret

In your garden, you can own all the land you want on your ocean, with a breathtaking mountain view. Plant as many trees and flowers that will fit; invite butterflies to flutter in the breeze. You can have it all right now *for free;* pay no taxes. No one can take it away from you. Live there full-time or travel there as often as you wish, without reservations. *I go there often, even for just a few seconds to collect my thoughts.*

Do you enjoy the quiet comfort of a secluded lake, the wondrous excitement of crashing ocean waves, or the stunning natural beauty of the mountains at sunset? What is your favorite tree – a weeping willow, white paper birch, maybe a flowering magnolia? How about a favorite flower – carnation, rose, or an exotic purple iris?

Smell is the most powerful of our five senses. Does the aroma of freshly baked bread make you hungry, or do you still savor the fragrance worn by your first love? Does the sweet perfume of blooming lilacs take you back to your grandparents' farm?

Do you hear the sounds of birds singing or a gentle breeze passing through the leaves of your favorite tree? Does the musical dance of wind chimes comfort you?

Let your mind create the environment of your dreams. Go ahead and add the shiny red sports car parked under the trees, next to your 40-foot boat moored in the lake with tiny ripples of water lapping against the shore. Make your garden so wonderful and tempting that you will never want to leave. This is the land of your spirit. Are you ready to own your private paradise?

Take several deep breaths and feel yourself relax. Taking deep breaths is a natural way to relax brain tension by adding oxygen (good energy) and releasing carbon dioxide (bad energy).

Pant Secret

Deep breathing is important and useful. "Just take a deep breath!" is a phrase probably ingrained in your head from a young age.

When an unexpected conflict is forced upon you, a deep breath buys you five or six seconds to gain composure. Not only does taking a deep breath give you more time to respond, but you're also oxygenating your brain to fuel intelligent, clear thinking – a vital component of decision-making. It helps you to return to, or stay in, your garden.

Do it now! Close your eyes, take deep, slow breaths for one minute and enter your private garden.

Escape to your beautiful environment as if you were sound asleep, without a single negative thought running through your mind. Hear the birds ... see the water ... your deep breathing is the wind that rustles the leaves in the trees. Relax, and your safe harbor will protect you.

Whenever you feel negative energy: anger, loneliness, jealousy, envy, or sadness, return to your garden as quickly as possible. Flush out the bad energy and replace it with positive; *it will only take a few seconds* to return to your happy land.

There has been an abundance of research linking positive thinking to living a longer, happier life. According to an article by the Mayo Foundation for Medical Education and Research, there are many health benefits associated with optimism, including decreased stress, greater resistance to catching the common cold, a sense of well-being, a reduced risk of coronary artery disease, and better coping skills during hardships, just to name a few. So why not start now?

Pant Secret –

Face adversity only when your mind and spirit are in the safety of your garden. When you do this, negativity will *never control* your life again.

"Most folks are about as happy as they make up their minds to be!"

~ Abraham Lincoln (1809 - 1865) ~

Pant Check Two

Earning Respect

Before you read the next section, please indicate how you feel about your ability to Earn Respect from others at/in:

	LOW				HIGH
Home:	**0**	**1**	**2**	**3**	**4**
Work:	**0**	**1**	**2**	**3**	**4**
Social Settings:	**0**	**1**	**2**	**3**	**4**

Today's Date: ______________________________

Happy Soles Make Happy Souls

Pant Principle – Look Like a Winner

Required Attire – Fancy Pants and Spiffy Shoes

Many don't realize the impact fashion choices have on their ability to earn respect. Image speaks volumes about credibility, poise, and confidence ... all before you even open your mouth. Looking polished and professional is an instant path to earning respect. When you look your best, you feel your best, and confidence radiates.

Though you get only *one* chance to make a first impression, second, third and future *consistent* impressions are just as crucial. In fact, with more people recognizing the importance of positive impressions, it's no wonder the image consulting business is now a booming industry.

"Good clothes open all doors."
~ Thomas Fuller (1608 - 1661) ~

Not sure how to dress to impress? The internet has 1000s of websites packed with great fashion advice and etiquette, right at the touch of your fingertips – and most of them are free.

Pant Secret

Dress as if you are going on an *important interview every day!*

Men – look around you. Take mental notes when you spot someone looking well put together. Invest in a subscription to a men's fashion magazine like *GQ (Gentleman's Quarterly)* for less than 20 bucks a year. It's a small price to pay for practical advice on today's fashion trends.

Women – you are much more fortunate in the fashion world. There are 100s of magazines with advice on fashion do's and don'ts for every occasion. Your favorite spa is a great place to peruse current publications to catch up on the latest fashion trends and accessories.

Pant Secret

It's impossible to change your height, age, race, or gender. However, there are plenty of things you *can* change to help you earn respect: your fashion choices, image, manners, posture, speech, and aspects of your health. Strive to be classy in any visible situation, whether it's at an important awards event or the grocery store.

Less expensive *doesn't* always mean less quality. If you're paying close to a grand for a suit, you're most likely paying for the designer costs and advertising associated with the designer's name. Forget it! The ticket to earning respect is all about looking neat, clean, and presentable – and it's easy to do at a price that won't break the bank. Be a savvy shopper! Join the mailing lists at your local department stores so you can be alerted of any upcoming sales. Shopping online is another great way to find designer fashions at a fraction of the price you would pay at the mall.

Looking sloppy or wearing clothes that are too tight or baggy with spots and holes doesn't give others the impression that you are dependable, respectable, or even competent. Wouldn't you feel better eating at a restaurant where everyone is clean, tidy and polished? Or visiting a doctor, lawyer, or other professional whose pants are pressed, shoes are shiny, and whites are bright?

Pant Secret

> The *fastest and easiest way* to enhance your self-image is to start from the bottom up. Or as many style icons say ... *"start with the shoes."*

Go ahead – take a look. Are your shoes scuffed, worn and dirty with rounded heels? Or are they polished, color-coordinated with your apparel, appropriate for the occasion? Every pair of shoes has something to tell. Do they show you walking with a spring and shouting, *"I am somebody,"* or do they show you dragging your feet? Stylish feet are happy feet! A sophisticated, classic pair of shoes is a step toward increasing your self-confidence and earning respect.

Why do you think the military demands spit-shined boots or shoes? It's because the military is the epitome of rank, class, respect, and leadership. Trousers and shirts are always pressed to perfection. Consistency is maintained throughout the ranks, from general to soldier. Even in combat situations, maintaining a polished look whenever possible is a source of pride and self-confidence and gives a sense of being in control. It's not about the appearance itself; it's about what the appearance *represents*. The military is building leaders, and leaders are formed out of discipline, class, self-respect, and respect for others.

Your shoes are the foundation upon which your character is built. They need to look good, fit well, and be appropriate for the occasion (you wouldn't wear wing-tips on the tennis court, but your tennis shoes should still look good and cared for.) When you feel good, it shows. Men – wear athletic shoes only when you are working out. They may be a fashion statement in some circles but are not for those who are wearing the pants!

Budgeting for shoes – and the rest of the look.

To get a quality pair of shoes that will look good for years, you'll need to spend at least a third more than usual. Get yourself a pair or two of "power shoes" – classic, timeless shoes that look great and feel wonderful. Find a store with a "shoe-smart" staff who can direct you toward achieving the proper look with quality built to last.

"It's always better to be looked over than over-looked."

~ Mae West (1893 - 1980) ~

Pant Secret

Ditch the jeans when trying to make a professional impression. *Blue jeans are the equalizer in fashion* and level the playing field for perceived image. Yes, designer, studded or embroidered jeans may give a slightly better look, but they are still your everyday basic denim. You earn respect by standing apart from the crowd, dressing with authority and conveying impeccable poise. There is a time and place for jeans, but appropriate and tasteful is always the rule in every situation.

Pant Secret – Get the Scent

Studies show a subtle hint of fragrance can lift your mood. Apply a *few drops* on your pulse points to not only improve your state of mind, but to also make a lasting impression on anyone you meet. *Don't overdo it!* It's better for others to *see* you arrive, not *"smell"* you around the corner.

Once you have those great shoes, work your way up – are your pants or skirts as nice as they can be? How about your blazer, shirt, and tie? Hair and nails? (Yes, men, nails are important as well – they should be clean, trimmed, and when you have a bit extra cash, even manicured.) Get great-looking, comfortable shoes and apparel: they all add up to a happy spirit and soul, which will draw others to like and respect you.

Pant Secret

When you look good, you feel good, and the effect is contagious. Wear those new shoes with pride and your feet will be happy. Happy feet turn into happy legs; happy legs turn into a happy upper torso, which lends its way to a happy head, giving you a *happy mind, body, and spirit.*

Those with great shoes have happy souls!

How To Break Free In a Snap

Pant Principle – Ditch Bad Habits

Required Attire – Rubber Pants

It's hard to respect someone while they're picking their nose!

Think you can't change your life in the course of a second? Snap out of it! In merely one swift moment you can *consciously* ditch bad habits that keep you from earning the respect you seek. Sound too good to be true? Read on. It's easier than you think.

Frank A. Clark once said, *"A bad habit is something you can do without thinking – which is why most of us have so many of them."* Just as Pavlov's dog was conditioned to expect food at the sound of a bell, we are blindly forming many of our behaviors and habits without knowing. Once the action is repeated over and over again, it forms a pattern and the behavior becomes subconscious and automatic. A habit is born.

Every one of us engages in bad habits hampering our growth in all aspects of life: emotionally, physically, socially, and professionally. Eventually, our bad habits become so deeply entrenched in our lives they become second nature. But think about this: aren't YOU the only one who can be held responsible for YOUR behavior? You and you alone have the power to form the habits that define you. Just as a bad habit can be formed, it can just as easily be broken.

Pant Secret

Those with the fewest bad habits earn the highest levels of respect. One of the *easiest* ways to gain respect and enhance your life is to *eliminate bad habits and replace them with good ones.* Let's talk about how.

"Curious things, habits. People themselves never knew they had them."

~Agatha Christie (1890 - 1976) ~

The first step in kicking a bad habit is *facing the fact it exists.* Remember the familiar saying "conquer your bad habits or they'll conquer you?" We make our habits, and then our habits make us. By identifying your bad habit, you're creating awareness by bringing it back into your consciousness. What are your bad habits? Are you even aware of them?

Pant Secret

One way to recognize your own bad habits is to become more aware of others'. Take for example using the overly-saturated phrase *"you know"* in conversations. Every time you hear someone utter these words, allow a "bell" to ring inside your head. From radio interviews to newscasters and general everyday conversations, many use this verbal crutch to the point of it diluting the message and damaging credibility in as much as 50% of their words spoken. Those bells in your head are ringing so loud you can't even hear what they're saying.

Most of our behaviors can be classified as habits. Do you have trouble making eye contact or find yourself with your arms crossed while having a conversation? If so, you're probably not presenting yourself in a position that earns respect.

Most forms of communication are non-verbal and body language is arguably the most powerful of all. Great leaders give off an air of confidence and earn respect largely from paying attention to what their body is saying. Strong eye contact, a firm handshake, and upright posture gives others the impression that you're confident and relaxed, and others will respect you for it. Develop these good habits until they become a pattern in your life.

Bad habits distract and irritate others and become their focus point of you. Good habits enhance how you are perceived!

Do you use improper language, interrupt others, complain or gossip? Do you have trouble keeping secrets? Are you an "I/me" person? Are you guilty of using *"um"* as a crutch in your conversations? How about the distracting habits of biting your nails, scratching, messing with your hair or face, nodding and saying *"uh-huh"* after every comment someone makes, or smacking your gum? The list is endless.

No matter how insignificant these bad habits may seem, they will come back to bite you. Here's your chance to recognize your weaknesses and extinguish them from your life once and for all.

Pant Secret

When you start hearing the words, *"Stop complaining"* ... *or "You could have it so much worse,"* it's time to snap out of this life-dulling negative habit. Otherwise, you'll never be able to wear the pants – *because they'll never fit!*

Step up to the plate and *focus on a solution* instead of whining about daily calamities.

Pant Parable

My grandfather was a wonderful person who treated everyone with the same respect. He was a farmer – slight but wiry, a very kind and funny man who never scolded or verbally corrected us. I fondly remember when he gave me attention in his own way, which was usually a gently pulled ear, one of his infamous "noogies," or a playful snap with a rubber band. But only in the past few years did I realize what he had done so effectively while we were growing up. He was correcting our behavior in a manner which we were unaware. He altered our bad behavior by taking our thoughts away from what we were doing. We stopped arguing, being rowdy, or whatever it was he did not like. Instead, we were distracted by Grandpa's little action that captured our attention. The technique worked! Rarely did we go back to the unruly behavior, because we were conditioned to learn new, "good" behaviors and to develop new good habits.

In keeping with the story I've just shared, I'm going to show you how to kick your bad habits just as my grandfather showed me. Focus on one bad habit at a time. Are you a knee bouncer? This habit is perceived as having a lack of concentration, low self-confidence, being nervous, and not being in control of yourself. (Not to mention, it's extremely distracting to others). If this is one of your habits, these negative characteristics may not describe the person you are today, but they may have been back when your habit was formed.

The habit I will break is:

____.

Stop reading right now and find a rubber band to put around your wrist. *When you strap it around your wrist, you will have my grandfather's spirit* to help break those nasty habits.

Order your *FREE habit-breaker wrist band, and bookmark reference guide at ... www.WhoIsWearingThePants.com*

Say out loud, *"I am going to break this habit starting now."* The next time your knee takes on a mind of its own, you must gently snap the habit-breaker and stop the bounce. In a short period of time, the snap will disrupt the ingrained habit enough times so that your brain will eventually become knowingly aware of your legs on the first twitch, thus breaking the pattern. Habit gone!

I have used my grandfather's trick to help me cut back on coffee, stop smoking, lose 50 pounds, and improve my grammar. I was guilty of committing one of the most common grammatical offenses: the use of the word "got" instead of "have" (i.e. I've *got* to get up early tomorrow). With just a few snaps, the words *must*, *will* and *need* have now permanently replaced "got" in my vocabulary.

Other bad habits such as *procrastination, over-eating, and lack of follow-through* are discussed in another chapter, but a good snap or two may be all the help you need to take control of yourself.

I understand having an elastic band around your wrist may look goofy. And sure, I know hurting yourself on purpose may seem a bit odd. But try this a couple of times and just the *thought* of looking goofy and being snapped may be the deterrent you need to break those habits. Think of your habit-breaker as if you are wearing rubber pants with its waistband as the perfect snapper.

What have your bad habits cost you?

Money? Advancement in your career? Relationships? Your health? You and *only* you have the power to change your destiny. *Snap out of it* – break your bad habits before they break you. You can't stay in the winner's circle for long if your habits annoy those about you. And don't even think about a casual "pick!" Protect your *perceived image* by eliminating these habits and your circle of influence grows larger.

Bad habits are easier to abandon now rather than later.

Enter a Popularity Contest

Pant Principle – Be Likeable

Required Attire – Comfy, Down to Earth Khakis

To many, the idea of a popularity contest may have negative connotations. I'm sure you have a few nightmare stories you can recall about the awkward "post-child/pre-adult" phases you experienced during your school years. Remember all of the melodrama ... the angst ... the cliques? These circles were so closely formed it was nearly impossible for an outsider to penetrate the shell of exclusivity. It was difficult *not* to be jealous, so we non-clique folks poked fun of them to hide our envy.

As time passed, we realized many of those kids were not *likable,* nor were they respected; in reality, the only reason they happened to be in the "in crowd" was because they possessed something desirable – looks, money, athletic ability, or influential parents. By the time I graduated from high school, my desire to be "accepted" into the popular group was the farthest thing from my mind. On the other hand, a *likeability* factor I deemed a very valuable asset. Likeability is another trick in the magic bag to earn respect. You do not necessarily have to like someone to respect them, but it sure helps!

According to a Gallup poll conducted prior to every presidential term since 1960, likeability has been the ONLY consistent determinant of the final election result.

Ultimately, likeability correlates to respect. If you feel a connection with that person and share the same beliefs and goals, you're more likely to give them your respect. It works just as easily the opposite way. If your likeability factor drops, your respect levels will shadow it.

Pant Parable

As was true for many kids, my eighth year in school was a difficult one. The "growing up" stuff was tough. One day I was approached by a pretty girl who happened to be a member of the "in" crowd. Charlotte handed me a note and invited me to her party. WOW! I was going to a "cool" party. The event was three weeks away and I thought I would burst from the excitement.

Saturday night finally arrived and I knocked on her door. I was feeling good in my new "madras" shorts with matching shirt, and I just knew it would be the best night of my life. When Charlotte opened the door, she had a puzzled look on her face and my heart stopped beating. I looked into her house and there were no kids! Was this a cruel joke? Were kids hiding to jump up and surprise me?

Then my ears heard, "Hi Dave, can I help you?" "Can you help me?" I thought, blushing to the roots of my hair. Why don't you just shoot me and put me out of this misery, I thought.

I heard myself say, "The party?" She laughed and informed me I was a week early and I should come back the next Saturday. This was not the kind of thing a teenager wants to have happen. The following week at school was pure torture! I believed every snicker I heard was directed at me.

The day of the party arrived and I didn't want to go. My mother talked me into it, assuring me everything would be fine. Well, it wasn't. It turns out I was invited to the party to be the date of a girl whom no one else wanted to date. I had been tricked, manipulated, and used. Charlotte wasn't so pretty anymore, and I lost my respect for her immediately.

That was when I began to learn there was a huge difference between *being popular* and *being likeable.* Popularity is more about status, fame, esteem and recognition. Likeability relates to human behavior and the qualities described as Pant Principles in the first chapter. But I also came to learn that when you're at the top of the likeability scale and you're winning the popularity contest, you'll find out just how fast your respect levels skyrocket.

Wearing the pants is *earning* the right to become popular by being a likeable person. Nothing happens overnight. Just like any other process, likeability is a skill set that must be pursued by following the Pant Principles. In this chapter, winning the popularity contest includes being likable.

Pant Secret

Life is a series of popularity contests. Think about it. Every president, military leader, successful teacher, Oscar winner, and others who have won elections or awards have all won popularity contests among their peers.

Be a "Big Pie" person. Do not be not afraid, jealous, or envious of someone getting a bigger slice than you. Believe the pie is big enough for everyone, and you can always find your share. I use this analogy to refer to someone else having good luck, achieving a promotion, getting a new car, or tying the knot. Be happy and express your joy to them – and make sure your feelings are *genuine* because your face will show your true colors.

Does everyone need to like you? Of course not! All you need is the support of at least 51% (majority) of your circle of influence. Great leaders have always had those who did not like or support them. However, those dissenters were outside the circle, or in the minority.

Leaders may make decisions that make little sense to everyone else. Perhaps a decision some would consider selfish, dangerous, and maybe not in their best interest. Overcoming a fear, taking time for mental adjustment, or temporary isolation are a few measures a leader may deem necessary for his or her own self-improvement.

Only the leader understands that the outcome of these actions will ultimately benefit those in the majority by making the leader stronger, happier or healthier, and positively impacting the majority as a whole.

Pant Secret

Trying to win the popularity contest does *not* mean being a pushover, nor does it mean being overly aggressive or violent. Wearing the pants is all about being assertive and self-confident while still showing respect for others. Leave aggression to the bullies.

Being likeable also requires sharing glory with others. We have all known someone who has reaped the praise from stolen ideas. Have the self-confidence to give credit where credit is due. Even better, give credit to those who need a boost in self-esteem, and you'll find a friend for life. It is easy to give genuine praise to the "efforts" of your family, friends and co-workers. Doing so makes them feel good and respect is sure to be returned.

Sometimes giving a pat on the back is difficult, especially when the effort may have been 90% you and 10% someone else. Understandably, it is foolish to grab all the attention for yourself. Do you know when you are hogging the glory? Are you an attention donor or a vampire of attention? Let's see.

Pant Test

When someone is giving information about themselves, are you:

REALLY ***listening*** and thinking about questions to ask back in order to learn more? Are you going to say, *"That is really interesting, tell me more about it"?*

This would make you an "Attention Donor."

Or ...

Are you ***just hearing chatter***, as if it's background noise? Perhaps thinking ahead of what to say when they are finished? If you hear your mouth saying, *"Let me tell you what happened to me,"* you are an "Attention Vampire."

Which are you? Knowing which type you are is critical to earning admiration and winning the personality contest. Not sure of your answer? *Listen to yourself* the next time someone tells a story. Your response will give you your answer.

Attention Donors give others the opportunity to receive attention. Attention Vampires need to suck up ALL attention for themselves.

Pant Secret

Attention Vampires *never* win a popularity contest, or the respect attached to it!

When a vampire reveals its identity, quickly change into your Bite-Proof Pants (that you will soon learn about) and *stop them from sucking all the attention out of the room.*

When the attack begins and you hear, "Well, let me tell you about ... me," politely state, "*Just a second, I want to learn more about what _______ was saying!*" Put the attention back on the person who deserves it and your respect will abound.

By the way, I happen to know a lot about Vampires, as in my life I have a tendency to want to share many of my stories. However, I practice every day to be an Attention Donor, working one step closer to winning the popularity contest.

Pant Secret

When you wear the pants, treat *yourself* as you want others to treat you. Like who you are and the accomplishments you have obtained.

When you respect yourself,
the need to declare your greatness
will disappear.

Pant Secret

Act happy! Fake it 'til you feel it! No one respects someone who is jealous, short-tempered or whiny. Your problems are yours to keep SILENT. Practice smiling right now. Feels good, doesn't it? The next time you attend an event, try this. Pick a place where no one can hear or see you, laugh out loud and exclaim, *"This will be so much fun. I can't wait to enter this room!"* When you walk through the doors, your cheeks will be rosy, your eyes will sparkle and your step will be perky. By making this your habit, you will become a people magnet, you will be respected for your positive mental attitude, and you will feel happier.

Have you heard someone say, *"Stay away from me – I'm crabby today?"* When *you* are feeling this way, never show it, and never announce it. Use this quote as a reminder as you try to win the popularity contest.

The only time people want to deal with a crab ... is when they want to eat one.

Pant Secret

Here's a trick about smiling and *emulating happiness.* Put smiley faces on your telephones. Every time you speak on the phone, have a smile on your face – with an especially big smile *when you end the call.* The person on the other end will actually hear happiness in your voice when you smile while you're speaking.

Pant Parable

My uncle Paul is one of the most likeable people I have ever known. He has a great deal of success in life and always wins the popularity contest. He makes people smile, even if they were out-of-line and needed a scolding. One of the most impressive attributes is the way he can supervise or give guidance. He usually says, "I know you already know this, but the correct way to say/do/think is..." This approach made me feel open about accepting his advice. He implied I was just forgetting the right manner of speaking or acting and always made me feel good about myself.

Try it – it works!

Every single day, give compliments and show appreciation. Be generous and don't hold back. *"You did a great job." "You look nice today." "Thank you for the delicious meal." "I really appreciate your help."* Gratitude will be remembered and will influence positive behavior in the future.

Be likeable even when you are feeling tired, sad, or blue. Smile and "fake it until you make it." Start collecting those votes!

Stand up for the people in your circle. Always make them look good to others, as you want your supporters to make you look good as well. In the next chapter you will learn a simple test to determine who your true supporters are.

When you support those who are not present, respect is undeniable from those who are.

Pant Check Three

Retaining Respect

Before you read the next section, please indicate how you feel about your ability to Retain Respect at/in:

	LOW				HIGH
Home:	**0**	**1**	**2**	**3**	**4**
Work:	**0**	**1**	**2**	**3**	**4**
Social Settings:	**0**	**1**	**2**	**3**	**4**

Today's Date: ______________________________

Snakes in the Grass

Dream Crushers & Backstabbers

Pant Principle – **Practice Self-Defense**

Required Attire – Bite-Proof Pants

Sometime around 550 BC, Chinese thinker and philosopher Confucius formulated one of the earliest versions of the golden rule: *"Respect yourself and others will respect you."* But many times it's just not that easy. In some cases, you might find emotional baggage from others dragging you down, causing destruction both to your self-respect and your quest to retain respect.

Of course, we all have imperfections, vulnerabilities, and flaws. Some are physical but most are emotional, cultivated by past experiences and perhaps fears of the future. Some can be changed and some can't – usually because we *won't*.

Pant Secret

You cannot be responsible for other people's imperfections from the past. The baggage they bring today is theirs, not yours. Do not attach yourself emotionally to their problems, or you will NOT be able to discard your own.

By detaching yourself from their baggage, you'll make yourself stronger and gain the courage to stand up for yourself when respect levels are jeopardized.

We have all encountered people who discourage dreams, stifle success, and dampen the courage and respect levels of those trying to improve their lives.

Some are the so-called "Fashion Consultants:" those who ask questions like, "You're going to wear THOSE?, What are you thinking?, That color looks horrible on you," or otherwise try to impose their opinions on you, criticizing openly, while doing their best to make you feel inferior. These critics have the power to virtually wipe out your self-esteem ... but *only* if you let them. Have enough respect and faith in yourself to realize these types of people aren't allowed *any* control over your feelings and actions. You are in control of yourself in any situation.

Others can be "Negative Nellies." They might snipe at you because they're jealous of your confidence and charisma. Others just enjoy putting people down in an effort to raise themselves up. At work or at play, you've surely run into the nay-sayers who see the dark side of any situation – the eternal pessimists, the ones who say *"It can't be done, it's never been done that way,"* etc. They constantly undermine your greatest ideas and threaten your good work, all at *your* expense.

Then there are those wanting to rain on your parade. *"Big deal! Anyone could have done that!" ... or "Why on earth would you want to go there; how unexciting!"* Many of these types are afraid you may outgrow them and lose "control" over you.

I challenge you to keep your umbrella held high and leave those attempting to rain on your parade *to get wet in the puddles they created.* Just say, "*Thank you for your* concern." Let this protective shield help retain your levels of respect.

And we've all met the "Drama Divas" or the "Demanding Kings" who crave attention and hog the spotlight. It's all about them; there's no such thing as sharing center stage. These are the type that "demand" respect, and for this precise reason, they never get it.

Backstabbers are everywhere. In their world, there are no rules. And they *want what you have*: *respect!* All of us can account for the wounds we've suffered from these types of people.

Do any of these sound familiar? Of course, because they are around us in our everyday lives: colleagues, co-workers, even family members. But just because they may exist in our circles doesn't mean we need to allow them to absorb all of our positive energy. For the most part, they are clueless of the concept of *allowing* others to improve self-respect.

Pant Secret

Such toxic people – I call them "snakes in the grass" – are *threats to our personal well-being* and success, as well as to the success and unity of our various teams. Retaining respect *requires* finding and removing individuals who are detrimental to our success and happiness. Facing these foes *requires courage and swift action.*

There are two fundamental species of snakes in the grass, each destructive in their own way. The first type I call the **pet snake**, which is *seemingly* harmless but has the potential to cause serious damage. The majority of the time, such **pet snakes** *don't intend* to cause you harm. In fact, it's entirely possible they might like...even love you. But mark my words – despite their innocent façades, these **pet snakes** will stay true to their nature, biting without hesitation and often without warning.

The **pet snakes** are usually friendly and may even be somewhat supportive. But occasionally, such snakes will try to damage your self-respect by saying or doing something to hurt your feelings, embarrass you or make you look bad. Phrases like, *"You can't, you won't, you aren't,"* are the asphyxiating banter they spew. And when you see or hear someone gossiping or spreading rumors about another person, you know you've uncovered a **pet snake** in the grass. Know they will tattletale on *YOU* when the opportunity presents itself. This type pretends to respect you, when in reality they're just trying to get what they want.

Pant Parable

I once had an accountant on staff who was very supportive of me and my efforts and often told me what a great boss I was. Unfortunately, she constantly made mistakes on our payroll. Instead of taking responsibility, her usual excuse to the office staff was, "Well, Dave won't buy me the software to get it right!" Of course, one of my employees finally asked me why I wouldn't provide her with "adequate" tools to correct the mistakes. I was dumbfounded. How could she blame her errors on me? In fact, I had purchased the latest software available, but she didn't want to learn how to use it. I had already recognized her as a ***pet snake*** *from previous nips, but this bite was a dangerous strike for sure. Her attempt to protect her respect level could only be accomplished by reducing my respect from my co-workers. Even though I liked her and I felt really bad about firing her – she had to go.*

Pet snakes are great players of "the blame game." Some people constantly blame others or circumstances for their own failings or make excuses. When you're wearing the pants, you will certainly be the target of this bite.

Former first lady Eleanor Roosevelt said, *"No one can make you feel inferior without your permission."* Had I not eliminated this snake from my circle, I would have made her behavior acceptable, and the venom would have continued to spread throughout the office, and perhaps even to customers. My leadership role and respect level within the circle could have been placed at risk and perhaps I would not have been wearing the pants for long. If other employees saw she was blatantly disrespecting me and I didn't put a stop to it, I'd be sending a signal that this sort of behavior was acceptable.

Pant Secret

It is difficult not to feel envious at times, but when envy goes unchecked it becomes dangerous. As envy grows, so does the need to acquire the object of desire. In this case, the object is respect. You have it – they want it! And they will try to take it away at all costs.

The second species of snakes is represented by the **viper,** existing in all sizes, shapes and colors. The commonality they share is that their bite is meant to harm and destroy their victim. This second and more dangerous species is venomous, envious, and resentful of your status and success. Such **vipers** consciously want to hold you back from achieving your goals, to turn your hopes into despair. What makes them even *more* dangerous than **pet snakes** is their devious ability to remain completely concealed, but always ready to strike without warning.

Vipers are the snakes that will attack when you least expect it. They are more likely to start rumors, not just spread them. Rather than attacking you directly, they are more likely to go directly to your boss, spouse, teammate, best friend, or even to your family to spread their poison. They will spread their venom to anyone within reach, poisoning others with negativity and aggressively trying to steal your respect.

Pant Parable

Some time ago, after I had been promoted to a management position as team leader, I noticed a change in demeanor in some of the salespeople who had seemed to be my friends just the week before. A few were cold and very unsupportive of my ideas. Within a few months, comments of jealousy and statements like, "I should have received that promotion" were shared with me from those who did support me. Then came the ***Viper*** *Strike: the president of the company brought me into his office and showed me an anonymous letter sent to him. It claimed I was stealing from the company and had a warehouse full of company materials.*

I couldn't believe someone could be so ruthless. After several days of investigation, I was 99% sure who was responsible for the attack. Instead of confronting the ***viper****, I went straight into the president's office and demanded to take a lie detector test, with the* ***viper*** *present. After I shared my suspicions, the president agreed. As it turned out, the* ***viper*** *had not actually sent the letter, but knew who had. His wife was the queen cobra and he had furnished the fabricated lie to her. She mailed it! He was fired and my level of respect was protected. My integrity was never questioned again.*

Snake Detection Questions

Look around. Who are the potential snakes in your circle? Ask these simple questions and answer them honestly. Write your answers down to keep track. Now, ask these questions with *your name* in the blank space.

Does ____________________ (write in one person's name)

1. Always make you look good and offer support?
2. Sometimes make you look good?
3. Rarely make you look good?
4. Never make you look good and never offer support?

If you can't answer "yes" to the first two questions, you have uncovered a snake. However, answer #2 could be a ***pet snake****.*

List a few other possible snakes in your circle:

____

____

Wearing the pants means becoming aware of any snakes in *your* circle and *having the self-respect to deal with them. immediately.*

Pant Secret

Gardens can become a breeding ground for snakes. Snakes are attracted to "safe" retreats, as they can hide in the grass and strike when least expected. It is mandatory and *YOUR* responsibility to rid your garden of existing snakes and protect your border from re-entry. You will never feel at peace unless your garden is snake free.

Keep the Snakes at Bay

Pant Principle – Control Adversaries

Required Attire – Second Pair of Bite-Proof Pants

Dealing with snakes

Put on a second pair of bite-proof pants and take action by using these three methods for dealing with snakes in the grass. *The actions required to control them are easier than you might think.*

Snake exterminator

1) If you are in the position to eliminate this person from your circle of influence, do so right away. By not taking action immediately, the venom will continue to spread, negatively impacting your chances for retaining respect and affecting your credibility.

Snake catcher

2) When you are not able to eliminate the snake, distance yourself from him or her, so it's harder for them to bite you. Minimize interaction, and try to remove them from *your* environment. If the snake is one of your employees, have them work in a corner, like a cage: in isolation, away from the team, or from home. By isolating the snake, there's less chance for the venom to cause harm.

Snake charmer

3) Insulate yourself mentally by ignoring the snake's actions. Don't take things personally. This may be your only self-defense when dealing with a family member or co-worker over whom you have no control. Protect yourself while remaining *courteous*. Do not try to bite back; you will lose.

Pant Secret

> *Exclude snake "friends" from your party list.* If you are afraid of the reactive bite created by the exclusion, it's even more of a reason to quickly distance such people from your team. Others will notice the snake's isolation and (a) probably appreciate the absence, and (b) gain respect for you for showing courage, and (c) think twice about trying to bite *YOU*.

Wearing the pants means protecting yourself and those in your circle from snakes who mean harm. By demonstrating the following qualities, you have the power to keep these enemies at bay. Though any *one* of these traits on its own can control a few snakes, the powerful combination of *all three* ensures you will wear the pants in all situations. Become a snake exterminator! Keep practicing the Pant Principles and you won't have to worry about the next encounter with a snake.

1) Likeability

2) Respect

3) Fear

Likeability and respect are discussed in other chapters. Let's take a look at the concept of *creating fear* as it pertains to retaining respect. Wearing the pants means being able to create fear *without being aggressive.*

How is this possible?

Snakes rely on threats and intimidation to educe fear. The Pant Principles rely on courage and a few memorized responses to employ *the only fear all snakes possess.*

Pant Secret

Snakes' greatest fear is being exposed. They hate being discovered and when they are out in the open, a rapid departure will follow.

Don't deal with a snake by becoming one yourself. When a snake attempts to bite, do not retaliate. This will only create more resentment. You may be surprised, hurt, or shocked from the attack, but you must address the issue as soon as you recover from the bite. Maintain your self-respect and confront your attacker with poise.

Instead of retaliating with aggression, try this approach. Say something like, *"I was surprised to hear you say that and it made me feel bad. What made you say that?"* More than likely the snake will be caught off guard and retort with an *"I'm sorry, I did not mean to...."*

You could also use a simple, *"Your comment didn't make me look very good in front of everyone else."* By confronting the action rather than ignoring it, you have just established the fact that the snake will be held accountable for its actions that affect your stability and level of respect.

If a second strike occurs, respond with another non-aggressive statement like, *"I need your help in understanding something. Is there a problem between us that I did not know about? We need to resolve this issue, because these comments concern me and I want to maintain a good relationship with you."*

Similar responses can be used at home, school or with "friends" who make comments like *"You'll never lose those extra pounds!", "They won't like you; you just don't fit in," "Ha! HIM? Fixing a car? He doesn't even know what a wrench looks like!"*

I shared this defense in an earlier chapter, but it's so relevant, I want to reveal it again. If a snake says, *"You are too fat to wear that/do that,"* and perhaps you are a little overweight, reply with, *"You might be right, but it doesn't feel good to hear you say something like that!"*

Pant Secret

Most snake bites can be answered with a simple, *"That wasn't a nice thing to say. It's not like you to say something so mean!"*

The snake now knows you are aware of its presence and it is "out in the open."

Are you afraid to confront snakes? Consider this:

Your family enjoys playing in the backyard. You look out the window and spot a *dangerous snake hiding in the grass.* What do you do? Easy answer, right? You will do everything in your power to protect your loved ones and removing it from your yard is a *natural instinct.* Remember this instinct when facing a snake at the office, at home, or in your social circles, as they are just as *dangerous to your family* as the one in your yard. When your respect and credibility levels are threatened, so is your income potential, your circle of influence, and the respect of your teammates. Facing the snakes becomes easy when the outcome decides who wins: you or the snake. Which one is going to Live Healthier, Happier, and Richer? Let out a little shout – ME!

Pant Secret

> ***Caution:*** If you hold a position in which you have direct control of someone's future (i.e. teacher, drill sergeant, boss, or parent), it's quite easy to instill fear by using threats: *"Clean that toilet or give me 50 pushups", "If you don't have the report to me by Monday, you're fired!", "Clean your room or you're grounded,"* and so on. These position-based threats will only *force* them to fulfill the task by way of intimidation. More of a bullying tactic than a form of leadership, this destructive quality usually results in making the snake *more resentful*

Your circle of influence is a reflection on you. If you surround yourself with snakes or allow them to bite you and flourish in your environment, what does that say about you – and your ability to wear the pants in any situation? What does this say about your self-respect? How much do you have?

Pant Secret

> As you start wearing the pants and assuming greater responsibility for your life, your circle will continue to grow, and more snakes will emerge. It's important to be aware of this phenomenon and to respond accordingly when needed. Snakes in the grass are not interested in nobodies. So enjoy the notoriety when they emerge. You must be doing something right!

To gain respect and enhance your life, it's vital to encircle yourself with positive individuals who always score a one or two on the "Pants Snake Test."

Pant Secret

Liar, liar, *pants* on fire! You can't wear the pants if they are burning! Even those little white lies to spare hurt feelings can come back to bite you. "Do I look fat in these pants?" is a dangerous question with an even more dangerous answer. Try and be evasive. *"Do you think you look fat?"* If really pressed, stick with another question. *"Do you feel comfortable wearing those pants?"* You can even use the same technique with questions about Santa!

When wearing the pants, you cannot empower a liar to continue practicing deception. No one benefits – not you *or* the fibber. When confronted with an obvious lie *from someone in your circle*, it is your responsibility to inform them that you will not allow deception. A comment like *"Is what you just said true?"* will normally short-circuit the statement. And if you can find your roar (see next chapter), then bellow out, *"Don't lie to me!"*

Allow a liar to lie, and the lie will grow!

Focus on what you *can* control by dealing firmly and swiftly with snakes *before* they can bite. When they do strike (and they will), make sure you are protected with your bite-proof pants.

A positive environment, free of predators, is the best garden to enhance your life, grow your team, and build your success. By associating yourself with people who share your values and beliefs, your circle of positive influence and levels of respect will only continue to grow.

If I Only Had a Roar

Pant Principle – **Develop Courage**

Required Apparel – Bulletproof Pants

Pant Secret

It takes courage to wear the pants. How did you feel when reading about *Snakes in the Grass*? Nervous? Afraid? Did you think, *"I can't do that?" You are normal to feel fear.*

Do you remember the cowardly lion in *The Wonderful Wizard of Oz?* At first glance, one might take him to be ferocious and mean, but deep down inside the king of beasts was ashamed of being just a plain ol' 'fraidy cat. He was all roar, without the sharp teeth to back up his bite. Though fearful on the yellow brick road, he does show brief moments of bravery along the way and is finally awarded the greatest accessory of all: the badge of courage. But rather than using it as he should – to protect the innocent and defend justice – for a short time, the lion abuses his gift and becomes a big, bad bully always picking a fight. Over time, he comes to realize courage is not about being fearful, but rather about exhibiting bravery while confronting his fear on the inside.

The lion's display of fear and cowardliness, and later his bullying behavior, prevented him from reaching his ultimate goal – the gift of respect. His true reward was granted when others began to respect him because of his courage – *not* because he exercised aggression.

It takes courage to face the snakes. It takes courage to confront anyone trying to impede your progress. Most of the time you'll be caught off-guard by confrontations. It's also likely your "opponent" will have had a chance to prepare themselves for battle, which puts you at a greater disadvantage. So how do you gain the upper hand?

Courage does not require physical strength; it requires preparation. It's all in your head!

Courage is the voice inside your brain telling you to take a risk. Courage is reaching out when you don't want to. It's standing up and facing your fears. Courage is the *learned ability* to overcome the fear present in all of us.

You might be thinking, *"But I'm not big and strong like a lion! I'm afraid of confrontation. I'm afraid of what others think of me. I dislike being the center of attention. I would never think of tooting my own horn, even though I may have done a great job."* These thoughts are common, but the need to step up and accept responsibility, to become the go-to person, requires courage. The courage to say, *"I can do this. Let me show you I can complete this task." "Trust me!"* Without this courage within yourself, respect is difficult to retain.

Pant Secret

You don't need the wizard's help to get the badge of courage! Most of those who show courage are neither big *nor* strong.

That was my mom: not big, and not strong. Nevertheless, she had the heart of a lion, and a mighty roar to match.

Every superhero has a gift: whether they can fly, spin a web, become invisible, or turn to flames. But none of them can afford their superhero lifestyle without the proper protection. This protection, whether it's a cape, mask or cloak, gives them confidence so virtually *no one* can hurt them. What a wonderful path to courage! You now have your bulletproof pants to give you the same protection. Wear them with confidence and courage.

The cowardly lion wore his bulletproof pants on the inside for mental protection, and you can too. Here's your chance to try those pants on for size.

We have all witnessed courage in strange places. Sometimes these encounters are heartwarming. Picture the two-pound toy Poodle, viciously growling at a monstrous Great Dane. The bigger dog could probably crush Foofie with his left paw without so much as a blink, but the ferocity of the tiny dog instills fear and uncertainty in the Dane and causes him to back away. Was the mini-dog courageous, over-confident, afraid … or just plain stupid? Probably a combination of all four! A firm stance, a snarl, and a fierce determination never to back down – all of it worked together to retain respect.

Was the smaller dog being aggressive or assertive? Had he tried to bite and physically harm the larger dog, he could have been classified as aggressive, which could lead to more serious trouble down the road. If he was simply defending his territory without attacking, we would call the dog assertive.

Pant Parable

Such is life. Audie Murphy, military hero turned actor, was the most decorated US soldier in World War II. At the age of 17, he wanted to enlist in the Marines, but due to his small, 5 ft. 5 in, 130-pound stature, he was declined. The Air Force paratroopers wouldn't take him either. Reluctantly, he settled for the Infantry, but it took only one battle to prove he was a courageous soldier despite his size and age. By the end of the war, his courage under fire won him 33 awards and medals, including the Medal of Honor, three from France and one from Belgium, all before he reached his 21st birthday. How's that for courage?

The kind of courage it takes to wear the pants does not generally pertain to life-or-death decisions. In fact, there is little chance of facing physical harm by being courageous. Courage is within *all* of us; we need to find it. And it can be learned quickly.

Pant Secret

Fear and uncertainty will never completely go away. Those butterflies in your belly, sweaty palms, red cheeks, the short breaths ... all of these physiological reactions to stressful situations *are entirely normal.*

Can you remember a time in the past when you wanted courage more than anything, but you just couldn't muster it up no matter how hard you tried? The word *coward* is a very strong label – as well it should be! You were a coward. Say it out loud, *"I WAS A COWARD!"* Do you remember how you felt at that moment? How about two hours later...even two *months* later? And how do you feel about it now? Probably not much better.

The two worst things about being a coward:

1) It feels shameful, depressing, and really bad.

2) People will not follow a coward; they can't trust where they will lead them, and they certainly will not respect them.

Now reverse the thought. Recall a time when you displayed courage. You stood up for someone or fought for something you believed in. You slipped into those bulletproof pants and boy did they fit great. How did you feel? Wonderful, uplifted, proud, and very strong. You felt good two hours later ... two months later ... and still today, the memory is glorious. These positive emotions should be reason enough to learn to overcome fear with courage.

Wearing the pants is not about being aggressive, spiteful, or malicious. In addition, it is not about *being* strong, but about *feeling* strong and displaying courage. When you wear your bulletproof pants, there is no choice but to be courageous at *all* times.

Sticks and stones may break my bones, but words can never hurt me.

This may have been the childhood mantra we spat at our enemies on the playground, but as adults it didn't take long to realize *this was far from the truth.* Words can undeniably weaken the strength and position of respect by eroding the foundation, as water is stronger than rock over time. Those in the circle witness these verbal attacks and observe the leader's response. If the leader doesn't practice self-defense from the snakes in the grass, how can those in the circle perceive him or her as anything more than a coward?

Start now to develop courage by standing up for yourself at all times. Be assertive. Listen to your inner voice and give your mouth permission to state your case. Keep your voice calm but firm. The people around you are not mind readers. They hear through their ears, not with supernatural abilities. If you take the offensive stance and vocalize your position, you'll discover the courage you have just demonstrated will usually outweigh the other person's will to continue the conflict.

Certainly, I am not suggesting you try to get a villain or criminal to back down by showing your assertiveness. Whenever physical danger is involved, it's usually best to choose an "exit strategy." Remember the familiar saying: fight or flight? It is actually a stress-response that happens in your brain and nervous system, not just a saying. Unless you or your family is in imminent danger, it's always better to choose flight.

Pant Secret

> You probably know that cuts, bruises, and broken noses are very painful and take a long time to heal. Walking away from a fist fight is not being a coward; it's being smart!

Let's add a third alternative to fight or flight: *"warning."*

Just as a rattlesnake's warning will usually deter an advance, you can be assertive without being aggressive. Wearing the pants is all about being assertive and self-confident, not aggressive or violent. As we have discussed in a previous chapter, sometimes this fine line is controlled by facial expressions, body language, and the tone of your voice, and can ***indicate a warning without saying a word.***

Wearing the pants is not only about standing up for yourself and your values; it also means standing up for people within your circle. It is your responsibility to stand up for your followers.

When a negative comment is made about one of your teammates, correct the attacker. When you are with a group and someone skips in line in front of you, it is your responsibility to show courage and politely inform the "skipper" where the end of the line is formed. At a restaurant, when the wrong food is served to someone in your party and the waiter insists this is what was ordered or to keep the item because it is "better" than what was ordered, *insist in a polite manner* to *"please bring the correct meal."* What a quick and easy way to earn and retain respect.

Of course, there will be times where your leadership role is not in jeopardy and the challenge really doesn't matter. You may choose to ignore the issue, but beware: it is easier to bypass a conflict than it is to address it.

However, self-respect is always worth considering. Why not take advantage of these opportunities to practice by using different approaches to find a win-win solution for everyone? Put on your bulletproof pants and be the hero. Learn to communicate your way out of a bad situation, or at least to diminish it!

Pant Secret

Courage is not about winning or losing; it's about doing the best you can to *fight adversity.*

Courage is standing up to sickness and life threatening diseases like cancer, ALS, or Muscular Dystrophy. It is not to dwell on what you cannot control, but rather to exclaim, *"I'm going to fight with every breath in my body!"* If the illness overcomes your body, it will not reduce your courage. Draw strength and courage knowing your spirit will live on with your family and friends through wonderful memories.

Courage is to overcome those feelings of jealousy and insecurity without punishing those around you. When someone stops wanting to spend their time with you, it takes courage to realize it's not about *you.* It's about *them* not being worthy of your affection. This kind of courage creates the highest level of RESPECT and will never fade or tarnish with time.

Pant Secret

You are already a superhero to someone in your life. It's time to expand the circle and earn respect from others.

Now ... GROWL loud as you can ... ***Growl!***

Not LOUD enough ... come on, *do* it!

GRRRRROOOOOOOWLLLLL! Now *that's* more like it!

If you are ready, then courage is ready! Slip into your NEW Bulletproof Pants of courage and never take them off....

Mow Your Grass on Thursday

(When no one is noticing)

Pant Principle – **Manage Time Effectively**

Required Attire – Invisible Pants

Pant Secret

With respect comes importance. Others will rely on you to be available when needed. *To retain respect, you must be there when expected.* To do so, there is another very important item you need to protect – your time.

Here's how:

Remember the classic film *The Invisible Man*? Based on H.G. Well's original novel, this successful adaptation spun off an entire series of copycat films involving the concept of invisibility. For the characters in these movies, invisibility was a superpower. They hid from their enemies, spied on the unsuspecting, and had the ability to attack undetected.

Have you ever thought about what invisibility could do for *you*? Now's your chance to reap all the benefits of this great superpower, and the best part is you'll retain respect by using the many benefits of being invisible.

Make a mental list of the many tasks aside from work needing to get accomplished: doctors' appointments, professional services, auto maintenance, errands, going to the gym, etc. I will refer to these tasks as "mowing the grass." It's not an ideal way to spend your time, but it has to get done. The important question is ... WHEN?

Carl Sandburg said, *"Time is the coin of your life. It is the only coin you have. And only you can determine how it will be spent. Be careful lest you let other people spend it for you!"*

Take a look at your weekly schedule and determine the most crucial times of the week to be present, accountable, and more importantly, the *least* crucial!

This chapter is not about cheating your employer or shirking responsibilities. Rather, it is about managing your time to accomplish your personal to-do list and still retain the level of respect from your peers. If you are paid for 40 hours, then give the best 40 hours possible.

If you are the boss, give your employees more than they give you. Your invisible time must be sheltered to ensure your *perceived image* is always being there for them. And, never discuss or divulge vacations. "Small pie" people dislike supporting your free time.

Establish your invisible day

Pant Secret

Mow your grass at a time you *won't* be missed.

For me, I choose Thursday – because this is the least important day and a perfect time for me to *become invisible.* My career has mostly taken place in a business-to-business (B2B) environment, holding the standard Monday through Friday, 8 to 5 weekday schedule. Monday mornings and Friday afternoons are the best times to be visible, since no one else wants to be. Tuesday is thought to be the most productive day of the week and Wednesday is "hump" day, so Thursday it is.

You must decide the most opportune time to make yourself invisible – when you are least needed. Whatever your day is, I will refer to it as Thursday.

Let's face it: juggling our careers with our personal lives can be a daunting task. Being a good time manager and leader means knowing when it's time to put on the invisible pants to complete those personal tasks. Earn that "free" time by buckling down when you are visible to create the space you need to get the "little" things done. This will prove to others that you are a person they can respect. Once you've established trust, others will not be keeping an *eye* on you, and you won't be missed.

Establish Monday as your opportunity to set the tone for the week. If you play too hard over the weekend and Monday morning is rough ... tough! Get really spiffed up; wear your nicest clothes. Be the first person to arrive at work. Be *happy* it's Monday. After all – it's the first day of the workweek; it's the first day to achieve new opportunities. Wake up motivated and make it the best week yet.

Pant Secret

Spread positive energy by expressing your enthusiasm for the start of the workweek. We often hear people complain about Monday. Every Friday exclaim, *"I can't wait for Monday!"* And on Monday, put your own twist on the familiar TGIF favorite by exclaiming, *TGIM!* (Thank Goodness it's Monday).

Money Day

If you work in the business-to-business environment, Tuesday is considered the most productive day of the week. Consider Tuesday your money day. Put forth your full effort on things that matter. Don't waste time on simple tasks like organizing, filing, or easy projects that can be completed on a Friday. Never take personal calls on money day. Every minute counts on Tuesday.

Look over your entire week. For instance, if you're in the boat-selling business, maybe your money day is Saturday, when many of your customers are seeking to enhance their leisure time. That's the day you put on those knee-pads and apply elbow grease, while everyone around you is wearing shorts and sandals.

If you're a stay-at-home parent, you might pick Wednesday as your money day, the "no-nonsense, get-things-done" day. If you're a student, choose one day a week when you focus 100% on your studies.

Or, if in the food industry, you may need to determine daily money hours, to practice perfection and enthusiastically complete your most important tasks. Pull out a calendar and write down *your* money times and attack your responsibilities with fierce determination.

Never promise more than you can deliver!

Choose your visible day

It is impossible to work 24 hours a day, 7 days a week. People who wear the pants must spend time securing the *perceived* image of always being visible when it counts. This begins the cycle of earning and retaining respect. If you can't prove you're a team player, the process has a difficult time starting.

Pick a time to be around when no one else wants to be. It might be doing something out of the ordinary at home or picking up a friend whose car won't start. Volunteer at a local food pantry or soup kitchen. At the office, be on time. Better yet, be early! Offer to help others get their projects done on time if they're lagging. Be there on Friday afternoon until closing.

Pant Secret

By being visible when no one else wants to be, you're building respect by developing a reputation of being dependable and reliable. Do what you say and say what you do. By doing so, you're making it much easier to become invisible when your Thursday comes around.

Wearing the pants and retaining respect through effective time management requires the following:

***Always* be there when needed and expected.**

Accomplish more than required.

Be skilled at what you do.

Most importantly – do it with passion!

Pant Secret

Be passionate! A salesperson, student, athlete or parent could have all the raw talent in the world, but *without passion it's difficult to excel*. Passion for your endeavor will give you that extra nudge to become the best. You do not have to be the best to earn respect, but as long as you're *striving* for it, you will.

Pant Parable

One of my early triumphs was directly related to a potentially career-ending moment. I was a salesman for an international company, attending a tradeshow in Chicago. Mid-week, several co-workers and I decided to go out on the town to release some stress. Before long, my watch indicated it was 4:10 a.m. I needed to be back in the showroom in less than four hours. Just after I glanced at my watch, I spotted the president and national sales manager sitting quietly at the bar watching our antics on the dance floor. I smiled, waved, and headed back to the hotel.

My dilemma: do I get two hours of sleep and risk not waking up in time? No way! This is my Money Day – a day to be very visible!

Despite the pain, I showered, dressed and had breakfast, without sleeping. I wanted to be the first person to arrive at the trade show and the last to leave – and I was!

And guess what? Not one word was said to me about the late night. Maybe my "work hard, play hard" mentality paid off.

Fast forward three weeks. I was summoned back to Chicago from Indianapolis to meet with the National Sales Manager. The flight was less than an hour, but seemed like a week. I thought for sure my chances for a future with my job were kaput.

Imagine my surprise when instead of being released, I was offered the position of Division Manager, becoming the youngest manager in the company's 100-year history. I later learned the company president had been evaluating how I fulfilled my obligations at the show, and was well aware of the pain and suffering I endured for 10 hours after my night on the town.

With this one decision, I officially launched the cycle of retaining respect with my employer. Who could dispute the fact that I could be trusted? By the way, I'm sure the president also knew that I had not divulged the fact I had seen *him* around town at the crack of dawn. Whoever said there had to be all work and no play?

Always exceed expectations!

When your circle begins to understand that you can deliver when it matters, they know you can be trusted to meet their expectations and your respect value becomes established. In turn, they will strive to earn your respect as well. They will want to follow your example and raise their own level of performance.

Guess what? You will soon be surrounded with respect-worthy people and your circle will get stronger by the day.

When you are mowing your grass on Thursday, smile and think, *"No one can see me on their radar screen with my invisible pants. I can enjoy this moment all for myself and retain respect at the same time!"*

Be the first to show, the last to leave, and invisible in between!

Pant Check Four

Giving Respect –

Before you read the next section, please indicate how you feel about your ability to Give Respect at/in:

	LOW				HIGH
Home:	**0**	**1**	**2**	**3**	**4**
Work:	**0**	**1**	**2**	**3**	**4**
Social Settings:	**0**	**1**	**2**	**3**	**4**

Today's Date: ______________________________

Selling The Pants Off Anyone

Pant Principle – Become Persuasive

Required Attire – Pants of Sincerity

"Me, a salesperson? Not a chance ... I don't have the right skill set and I hate to be sold!" Sound familiar? Or do you enjoy the selling process? In many ways, *selling* shares many similarities with life's everyday occurrences.

Wearing the pants often involves "selling" yourself, your ideas, your beliefs, and your actions in order to earn others' trust and respect. Think about what makes *you* important. What value do you hold? Are you a respected member of the group? In your family environment, do you cook, mow the grass, help with homework, entertain? At work, do you excel at what you are being paid for? In a social setting with friends, do you make them laugh? Do they feel good about being around you?

"Everyone lives by selling something."

~ Robert Louis Stevenson (1850-94) ~

You may not think of it this way, but all of your interpersonal communications are part of selling. Selling your value and selling *yourself,* that is. The only way you'll encourage someone to buy what you are selling (which is yourself) is if they look up to you, trust you and respect you. Trust your newfound courage to share your opinions with others.

Unfortunately the word "sell" often conjures up negative connotations: sleazy, sneaky, pushy, self-involved. Let's face it: stereotypical salespeople who fall into these categories are found in every profession from retail to insurance, real estate to telemarketing, and everything in between. We are so accustomed to their "bad rap" that we avoid taking on the stigma of "selling" – simply because we've been preconditioned to dislike it.

But in reality, it's not so much the selling process we do not like, but rather the "pitch," or how the selling tactics are delivered. We may view the pitch as a one-sided dialogue to trick us into doing something *we may not want to do.* When I get pitched by a salesperson, coworker or even a family member, my instincts go into *beware* mode and remain there until I feel *sincerity* and *respect.* Is the pitch-giver sincerely interested in *my* gain or simply his or her own personal gain? Do I respect and trust the person? Does the person show respect for my time, my resources, my intelligence?

Pant Parable

Recently I was shopping for a second car. As I pulled up to the showroom, my eyes locked with those of a slick-looking salesman, lurking behind the door, and ready to pounce. Before I could even open my car door, he was right there opening it for me. I kid you not; it felt like I was in a bad movie, scripted to highlight the most obnoxious, stereotypical salesman in the western hemisphere. He even proceeded to make fun of my Lexus, asking me if I was ready for a "real" car ... one that offered a far better value. He said he had an "incredible" deal on a red, Jeep Renegade, and then he had the audacity to ask if I was a cash buyer. And if he made me a good deal, was I ready to buy today? Believe it or not, all of this happened in less than sixty seconds! Remember those internal bad emotions we discussed in "Stay in Your Garden"?

Well, I had them all in high gear ... to the point that my ears stopped working, and I felt as if a bully was attacking. I pushed my way past him to the information desk and asked for the manager. Fortunately, the man behind the counter replied, "That's me. How can I help you?" A quick reflection of my mental garden relaxed me and I responded, "I would like to speak with a salesperson, but not him," as I pointed toward the "commission-breathing" vulture. He volunteered to personally help me in my search for the right vehicle. Now that's what I wanted to hear!

Pant Secret

By the way, *commission breath* is a pant term for pushy salespeople with a lack of sincerity and a plethora of arrogance, or when it's evident they are approaching me strictly for their own gain. It's as if they are desperate to make the sale and I can almost feel their breath down my neck as the pushiness begins.

I felt obligated to share (*not whine, bitch, or complain*) with management how I felt about my first impression of his business. I explained that I did not feel like I was being *given the respect* a customer deserves. Likewise, I would also want to know if someone in *my circle* was behaving in a manner that didn't positively represent me. I also believe that by bringing the salesman's poor behavior to management's attention, the obnoxious fellow might learn something about human behavior, and the meaning of *respect.*

Can you remember how your parents got you to do things their way? Did they exert direct control over you? Maybe they bribed you or rewarded you with something they knew you wanted. Was making you feel guilty a common strategy? Are you using the same tactics on your children, friends, and coworkers? There is a better way!

The Pants Approach

Instead of associating the word "sell" with negativity, look at the positive aspects ... like negotiating, consulting, listening, teaching and helping. As you're about to read, *selling* is such a basic concept and necessary element in life that we must adjust our mental picture of the word.

Pant Secret

In your mind, replace the term *"salesperson"* with *"Pants Coach."* After all, *Who Is Wearing The Pants?* is about following the **Pant Principles** and teaching them to others. What is more sincere than genuinely *wanting to help others gain respect, self-confidence, pride, and a positive attitude?* Plus, if you can inspire someone to do something that's positive, then you win too!

As creatures of habit, the majority of us do not like change – simply because our minds are apprehensive when it comes to the unknown. We are so habitually comfortable with our everyday routines that any kind of change (even if it's in our best interest) will cause anxiety levels to shoot through the roof. We have been mentally conditioned to distrust a salesperson's "pitch" and instinctively respond with *"No, thanks," or "I don't want to,"* sometimes without even knowing what they're trying to sell. When you enter a store *to buy something* and are asked, "May I help you?" do you normally say no?

In searching for respect, we cannot *force* or *trick* others into doing anything. It's a leader's mission to show how our proposal can make a direct, *positive impact* on the other person. We must be sincere and understand the subject's wants, needs, and desires. When a positive dialogue is established, we are one step closer to earning trust and respect. Then, people are more comfortable following our suggestions, resulting in a win-win for all.

"I am the world's worst salesman; therefore, I must make it easy for people to buy."

~ F.W. Woolworth (1852-1919) ~

Pant Secret

WIIFM – "What's in it for me?" is the million dollar question ... and influences every decision I make. A Pants Coach understands this need, providing the answer before the question is asked and never having to actively sell anything! It's really all about helping the other person and showing genuine interest and respect.

To illustrate, we need to understand how marketing differs from selling.

Marketing a product, service or concept is the vehicle to creating demand, or want, and need, to *motivate* action. It is the promotional pitch that helps make someone *want to buy* or *accept the advice* or *offer*. If a promotion provides enough appropriate WIIFM responses to create this demand, a salesperson is not needed. Wow, wouldn't this make life easy?

WIIFM's are the benefits gained when decisions are made or by following advice to:

Fulfill a need

Improve our lives

Make us look good

Make us feel good

Protect our families

Eliminate frustration

Save time or money

Well, what do you know? These are the *basic* benefits in life *we all* strive to achieve: professionally *and* personally. Finding and offering these benefits will persuade others to want to do what you ask, and not feel as though they are being manipulated. Create the want and need with persuasion and establish an emotional connection.

Pant Secret

> When leaders *inform* and *demonstrate* to others the benefits that will be obtained by following their advice, they have just become *persuasive.*

Here are a few everyday Pant Coaching examples:

"I hate school/studying/exams."

> *"I understand, but a better education will make your* ***life much easier*** *down the road. Think about* ***how good you will feel*** *when you are* ***rewarded*** *with all of your hard work!"*

"I do not want to eat peas!"

> *"Peas will make you* ***stronger and faster****. You do want to* ***run fast,*** *don't you?"*

"I can't remember to change the batteries in the smoke alarms."

> *"I would* ***feel so much better*** *and it would be* ***safer*** *for the family if you would remember to change them. Wouldn't you* ***feel good*** *about that?"*

Pant Secret

> *If* you are certain you'll be met with resistance, it is important to deliver the benefits *before* seeking acceptance.

> *"I would like to discuss with you the possibility of moving. It will be* ***good for the family****. We could* ***spend more time*** *with the kids. You and I will* ***have fun*** *and* ***play more*** *tennis and do* ***more traveling****. What do you think?"*

> *"Bill, you are late again with your project. This must be stressful to always be rushing to finish at the last minute. Why not* ***eliminate this frustration*** *and start on the next assignment right now? I'm sure you'll* ***feel great*** *about finishing early next time. You might even* ***save time*** *by starting now!"*

Decide today to be a Pants Coach and help people feel good about following your advice. At the same time, remember how powerful you can become as a "benefit finder," because without a reason to do something, nothing gets done.

In Napoleon Hill's book, <u>*Think and Grow Rich*</u>, there exists this quotation: *"It is as useless to try to sell a man something until you have first made him want to listen as it would be to command the earth to stop rotating."*

To prove how strong the art of persuasion can be by using benefits, examine these excerpts from a speech made to soldiers waiting to invade France.

General George S. Patton, Jr.
3rd Army Speech - England.
31 May, 1944 - 6th Armored Division

> *"Men, you are here today for three reasons. First, because you are here to* ***defend your homes and your loved ones****. Second, you are here for your* ***own self-respect,*** *because you would not want to be anywhere else. Third, you are here because* ***you are real men*** *and all real men like to fight. When you, here, every one of you, were kids,* ***you all admired*** *the champion marble player, the fastest runner, the toughest boxer, the big league ball players, and the All-American football players. Americans* ***love a winner....***
>
> *Now, there's one thing that you men* ***will be able to say*** *when you get back home, and you may thank God for it. Thirty years from now when you're sitting around your fireside* ***with your grandson on your knee, and he asks you****, 'What did you do in the great World War Two?' ... You know how I* ***feel****. I will be* ***proud*** *to lead you wonderful guys into battle anytime, anywhere. That's all."*

These same basic benefits are used in Patton's short speech, and no doubt it was inspirational. His men loved him, respected him, and followed him with great success across Europe, covering 600 miles in record time. General Patton ended the speech with the most important declaration a leader must make,

"I will lead you!"

Pant Secret

> It is easy to become the world's *best* salesperson by *giving respect* to the person on the other side of the table. Respect who they are, what they know, and the time they are giving to you. By doing so, you will be greatly rewarded and respect is reciprocated. Replace the term ***sales cycle*** **with *persuasion cycle.***

The customer may not always be RIGHT; however, they are never WRONG!

(and remember, the customer may be your child, spouse, boss, and even an adversary)

Practice makes perfect and it is time to put our thoughts together and become more persuasive. Be interested in a person's improvement and you will improve yourself.

You will arrive at a chosen destination, IF you are going in the right direction.

Direction in life can be altered in one second.

Just turn around and start moving the right way.

Coaching to Inspire

Pant Principle – Be a Mentor

Required Attire – Pants of Knowledge

If there's one quality above all others that will help you give respect, it's the ability to inspire others. As you continue to gather respect, there will be many opportunities to help others improve their lives. Apply the Pant Principles you've learned to real-life situations so you may pass them along to motivate others.

Where have your inspirations come from – family, friends, bosses, coaches, teachers, celebrities, world leaders? Take a close look at the people who inspire you. What is it they all have in common? Above all else, each of these people have *earned* your trust and respect.

***When you inspire others to think,
dream and do more,
you are wearing the
Pants of Knowledge.***

I want *you* to be one of the special people making a difference in the world, even if only to one person. Whether it's offering a helping hand, giving a voice to those who don't have one, or striving to set good examples, inspiration is the spark setting ablaze the desire to reach for the stars. *Inspiration is the foundation for motivation,* for without it nothing gets done. Those you inspire will help determine *your legacy in life.* It is my inspiration to inspire *you*!

Pant Secret

> Giving respect is not about domination or demanding respect, but rather about inspiring others to take action by following your attitude, actions, principles or ideas.

You can easily recall examples of *poor leadership*. We've all been victims. You know the type: the callous, the corrupt, the creeps, the arrogant! Look back at your experiences with the "bad apples" of the bunch. Sure, they may have accomplished their goal, but they left a path of destruction along the way, without giving respect to anyone. Hopefully, they inspired you not to make the same mistakes and to keep your pants clean.

If you want respect,
then you must give respect.

We have also known *incompetent* leaders or coaches who dissuade, inhibit, or disrupt teamwork. This person may have been *appointed* a leadership role without possessing the necessary skills, training and knowledge. They may rely on bullying tactics to abuse their power, and they rarely motivate anyone.

The bully on the playground, home, or office is not a leader. It is the leader who takes the power away from the bully!

Pant Parable

One of my first jobs was stocking the shelves at a grocery store. Being the new kid on the job meant I was assigned all the dirty work: cleaning the bathrooms, taking out the garbage and polishing the floors. And what in the world did I know about taking care of a floor at 15 years old?

When I expressed my concerns, my 17-year-old night supervisor (leader) provided his management wisdom. Here was the extent of my training, "There are big barrels of 'tile floor stuff' in the back storage room. Mop it all over the floor and make sure you are done before 5:00 am. It takes about an hour to dry and the store opens at 7:00 am!"

Boy, did I work my tail off. I made sure there was plenty of floor sealer everywhere. I worked on the project for 7 hours.

I fell asleep as soon as my head hit the pillow, drifting off into a dreamland of dollar signs, my mind's subconscious way of hoping I earned a raise. In my slumber, I heard the phone ring. Wow! That was quick ... the manager of the store must be really impressed! But when I said hello, the voice was anything but pleased. "What have you done!" he screamed. "When I opened the store this morning, my shoes stuck to the floor so tightly I could barely back out the door. Tell me what you did!" Once I explained the procedure I followed, he called me an idiot and fired me on the spot. Apparently I left out one very small detail – one that caused the store to close for 3 days. It took the help of a professional flooring company to rectify my mistake. Little did I know there was a second chemical that should have been added to the barrel to cure the sealer. Needless to say, the meaning of epoxy is now ingrained in my head just as solidly as the manager's shoes were to the floor.

The grocery store ultimately went bankrupt (not due to me I hope.) But looking back, it is easy to formulate its demise. There was no leadership from the top down, tasks were delegated to all the wrong people, and no one was inspired to care about the company's future. Most importantly, *no respect was given* or *received by anyone.* It was obvious the wrong person was appointed to a leadership role. I sure learned a lot about what *not* to do if I ever became the boss.

In my experiences, the majority of coaches have been *neutral* leaders, and usually appointed to a leadership position by default or time spent on the job. Most of my schoolteachers didn't strive to make a difference. They were there to pass on purely "textbook" knowledge and that was the extent of it.

However, many of the Pant Principles I'm sharing with you are a *result of my inspirations* from a few coaches who *did* make a difference ... people who earned my respect and gave me respect became those I *wanted* to learn from.

Pant Parable

In the ninth grade my math teacher, "Smokey" as we fondly called him, was likeable ... but boy, was he tough. No late homework, no chitchatting, no calculators ... it was strictly business in his classroom! I struggled with many of the formulas he was teaching, but each time I expressed my concerns, his reply was always, "Re-read the chapter."

One day I gathered my nerve and explained, "I have always been good at math, but I've studied the chapter and I'm getting nowhere." After a few seconds of eternal silence, he asked if I was willing to give up some of my free time. We only met a few times, but these meetings inspired me to remember him as a great mentor, for he forfeited his own free time to help me.

Continued ...

He taught me that math is not about the formulas, but rather about focusing on the process and the method used to achieve the end result. Complete the first step and the rest will follow.

Without pay, he gave me more than a solution to a math problem – he taught me an important lesson in life. ***Focus on the process!*** *He inspired me to use this lesson in all aspects of my life. Most importantly, he respected me as an individual and believed in my potential to succeed.*

Smokey earned his nickname because he volunteered his summers at the Forestry Department to live at the top of a tower and watch for forest fires in National Parks...ranger hat and all!

My definitions of those wearing Pants of Knowledge:

> One who inspires someone to *better* themselves.
>
> One who inspires someone to be, do, or act like a leader and *stand up* for what is right.
>
> One who inspires someone to help achieve and to pass on the beliefs and goals of the leader.

The common thread linking giving respect and leadership is the magical word: *inspire.* When a person inspires another, it changes both of their lives, just a little or a whole lot.

Mentors like Smokey would best represent the first type of Pants of Knowledge coaches. Anyone who has touched your life in a positive way, even if just for a few minutes, is a mentor. A mentor can even be a stranger who offered advice about throwing a baseball. The stranger had no hidden agenda. He wasn't paid for it and no one else benefited – just you. So why did the stranger do it? Because it made *him* feel good to help!

Pant Secret

> Being a mentor is easy to practice and requires only one Pant Principle – courage. It does not matter if a mentor is a good person or has integrity. The only thing that matters is he or she inspired you by helping to improve your life.

The second type of a Pants of Knowledge coach is less noticeable. This type of coach is one who walks the walk and talks the talk. He or she is someone you strive to be like. Some examples might be:

A father who offers to coach his son's baseball team when the coach calls it quits.

A friend who refuses to let you drive after a party where a couple of drinks were consumed.

A teacher who stands up for you when another student pokes fun.

A mother who helps you mend a broken heart by sharing her own similar experiences.

These coaches receive comments like, *"My dad's great, I want to be just like him when I grow up!" ... or "I will stand up for someone just like my teacher did for me."*

Type two coaches demonstrate how *you* can become a wearer of Pants of Knowledge by exhibiting the attitudes that allow you to succeed. Such leaders must possess, practice and preach the Pant Principles of:

Courage, Compassion and Integrity

The third and most visible type of coach is the one who inspires others to follow in their footsteps. Such leaders are usually charismatic and persuasive in getting others to share the same vision. Some of these have changed the course of history – for better or worse!

Many of us do not want the kind of responsibility associated with this third type of leadership role. However, everyday life requires teamwork, and someone needs to be in charge ... so why not you? And if *not* you, that's okay, too. Being the *best player on the team* is a form of guidance that's powerful in its own way. All three types of coaches *inspire others*. You can be any one of the three, **but why not strive to be *all* three?**

Pant Lesson

Think of three people who have touched your life in a positive way. Pick one from each category based on the three definitions listed above. List the *qualities* you admire about this person and the characteristics that earn your respect. How have they inspired you and what lessons have you learned?

(My Choices)

Mentor like: (Smokey)

To be like: (My Dad's calmness, my Mom's courage)

To lead like: (Uncle Paul)

From now on, practice and apply the principles learned in this book and mirror the actions of these three people. They are your role models. Formulated from their characteristics is born a *brand new you.* Always ask yourself, "What would 'the new me' do in this situation?"

Pant Secret

You know the old adage, "Do unto others as you would have them do unto you." Do you want people to listen? Then you must listen to them. Do you want people helping you look good to others? Then reciprocate and do the same.

Remember Smokey's lesson. Complete the first step and the rest will follow. *Focus on the process!*

Pant Secret

Act as a role model. *Do what you say and say what you do.* When you do, someday *your* name will appear on someone's "Like List," and they'll pass along your ideas and visions *you have inspired them* to believe in.

The power to inspire –

There's no feeling like it!

Pant Check Five

Putting It All Together

Before you read the next section, please indicate how you feel about your confidence in Wearing The Pants at/in:

	LOW				HIGH
Home:	**0**	**1**	**2**	**3**	**4**
Work:	**0**	**1**	**2**	**3**	**4**
Social Settings:	**0**	**1**	**2**	**3**	**4**

Today's Date: ______________________________

Board the Train

Pant Principle – Reach Goals

Required Attire – Engineer Pants

"All aboard!" Blow your horn as the platform clears and you settle in for the ride. On this trip, you are both a voyager AND the engineer. Excitement is in the air as you think about your journey to gain respect and your quest to fulfilling your dreams. Your mind clears of everything but the resonance of the train's gentle rumble as it rolls down the tracks. Sounds wonderful ... and it will be!

But there are things to take care of before you board. What is your destination? How long will it take to arrive? You don't want everyone to wonder where you are, so tell your friends, neighbors and family where you are going and how long will you be gone.

Without the planning process, what do you have?.. Simply a dream without the journey. As you would plan an important business trip or a once-in-a-lifetime vacation, the path to earning respect requires just as much attention to detail. Leave no stone unturned as you formulate your itinerary to eliminate as many obstacles as possible.

As the engineer of this train, the journey ahead is all yours to command. Take advantage of this newfound power and steer yourself down the right track. How it moves and where it takes you is completely up to you.

A plan is the journey to achieving the goal.
A goal without the plan is only a dream.

Pant Secret

Your dream *MUST* be achievable. Easy enough, right? Your parents have told you in youth, "You can be anything you want to be." True to a point – yet a bit destructive, too. In life, we all have *wants:* to be the quarterback of the football team, the head of the class, the one with the nicest car, most popular, best looking, etc. Disappointment was inevitable, and you began to realize you couldn't have everything you wanted. Maybe upon this realization, you slowly started to respect *yourself* for the person you truly were. Or, perhaps you felt despair!

Do you ever feel disappointed when you realize you're not living the life you've dreamed for yourself? Of course you do. It's *normal* to feel these negative emotions. It is also normal to become *more* discouraged about feeling discouraged. But who says you have to be "normal" anyway? Use your garden to dispel these bad emotions and don't become like everyone else.

Start by turning your *want* into a dream. Prioritize the order of your wants. To begin your journey to *earn* your dream, think to yourself, "More than anything in the world, I want ____________________________." If the want is unrealistic, the path may lead to disappointment.

Every astronaut once dreamed as a child of traveling to space. But those who shared the same dream and who did not achieve the goal, either a) did not have a strong enough plan, b) had no plan at all, or c) simply didn't board the train. By following your dream, you are showing courage and determination – the "good stuff" leaders are made of and respected for.

If you fail to plan, you plan to fail!

Pant Lesson

1.) Write down a dream you most desire to achieve: ______________________________.

2.) Determine the route or plan. Approach it as if you are taking a wonderful vacation. When does the train leave? The journey is the trip to achieving the dream and you won't succeed if you don't take the first step. You must decide when you are going to begin and write it down. ("Now" is the best answer.)

Train departs at: ______________________.

When does the train arrive at the destination, or when would you like to achieve your goal? How long will you devote to the journey? Be realistic and add 20% more time to allow for a few detours along the way. As the engineer, you decide the direction and speed of your journey.

Train arrives at: ______________________.

Are you physically prepared? After all, you certainly want to be able to enjoy the dream once you arrive. If your dream is to lose weight, what are the steps needed to achieve this goal? You should schedule a physical with your doctor for an overall health evaluation, learn about the proper diet for your individual needs and visit local health clubs to build up your stamina. Be precise: Do you want to *lose weight?* Or do you want to *remain fit for the rest of your life?*

During the course of your journey, you may have to transfer trains a few times to complete the trip. That's okay! This isn't an express train, it's a voyage filled with small stops.

Pant Secret

Just as you would boast about the dream vacation, *share* with your circle of influence the planned journey to achieving your goal. Occasionally you may need a boost to keep progress moving forward. Your circle may offer encouragement, but more often it will be *your* pride and courage shouting at you, *"Hey, get back on the train! Keep following the process. I refuse to be embarrassed by failing in front of everyone! Here's my chance to gain the respect I have earned."*

You're wearing your Engineer Pants now. Have confidence in yourself to take life by the reins. You're in control, with the opportunity to conquer every obstacle that faces you on your track. Be proud to wear those pants!

Along the journey, you'll no doubt encounter snakes in the grass, as they will slither aboard your train. *"Can't do that!"* they'll say. Draw strength from these comments. Let your inner voice laugh and think, "*Just watch me!*" Use the rules you have learned to overcome these burdens and respect levels will remain high.

Stay well-rounded! Having one big dream with a plan for getting there is wonderful, but surely there are other things to accomplish. Choose one dream for *every part of your life:* personal development, business, family, and one just for fun!

Living multiple dreams will enhance your journey, but also increase the probability of success in accomplishing your dreams, as you will feel good in doing so.

Become a doer by simply doing!

Sample Dreams List:

Personal Development – Learn to overcome fear of public speaking.

Step 1: Join Toast Masters organization. Within two weeks (commit to a date) ______________________________.

Step 2: Rid myself of bad speaking habits. Start today.

Business – Become more widely known in the local business community.

> Step 1: Join a Chamber of Commerce and attend meetings. Within one month (date) _____________.
>
> Step 2: Network at tradeshows and business luncheons. Within two months (date) ___________.

Family – Improve the health of myself and family.

> Step 1: Evaluate the current health conditions of each family member to plan a dream achievable for all. (date) ______________________________.
>
> Step 2: Discuss charity events for family participation (walks, runs, triathlon, etc.).
>
> Step 3: Register my family for the first event. (date) ____________________________________.

Just for fun – Take tennis lessons.

> Step 1: Visit local health clubs and interview instructors. (Date) ____________________________.
>
> Step 2: Join club and start lessons. (Date) ______.

And of course – Tell my *inner* circle of influence about my goals and dreams and when I WILL do them.

Pant Secret

It is *your choice* to feel *GOOD* about yourself. There is no better feeling than being on the train, looking out the window at all the dreamers still standing on the platform and wishing they had the same strength and confidence to board. As you pull away from the gate, some are waving, wishing you success. Some are smiling, but hoping you fail. Others remark how luck always follows you.

But only *you* will know how it feels to plan your destiny. To make your own luck. To not have to fear failure because you realize you will learn from your mistakes and gain strength in the process. To become the best person possible for yourself, and in doing so ... help everyone else around you. And most importantly, to earn respect by making wise decisions, acting with dignity, wearing the pants, and respecting yourself.

Wear your Engineer Pants with pride and never be without them. Be in charge of your route and become the best engineer the world has ever seen – even if you *are* the only passenger on your train via the journey to earning respect.

After you board your train and blow the whistle, it's time to push the throttle forward and let your journey begin!

WHOO! WHOO!

Note: If you did not fill in the above blanks for your dream and steps required to catch it, think twice about moving forward. Don't be left with only a dream! Why not catch it?

Earn Your Final Degree

Pant Principle – Have Commitment

Required Attire – Clean, Pressed, Well-Fitted Pants of Respect

On this journey, your baggage allowance is only *one* suitcase. Now that you have a full wardrobe of pants, take a swatch from each pair to bring with you. These swatches are the combined fabrics, woven together from your collection to represent your most important item of attire: Pants of Respect. Wear your Pants of Respect to remind you of all the practical tips, tricks, and secrets you've learned.

Hopefully, you've *snapped* away some of your bad habits, given your image a mini-makeover and, proven you've got the bite to back up the roar! And, you're talking the talk and walking the walk like a leader on a mission. It has been fun and exhilarating to share a few of my methods, stories and life experiences, and I hope you've enjoyed the little journey we've taken as much as I have. If I have influenced your life even in a small way, then I feel as though I've achieved a great deal.

Often, I'll catch a colleague, friend, or family member quoting references to this book under their breath. *"There's a snake in the grass,"* they'll mutter. Or, *"I need to get back into my garden."* Once I was pleased to hear a friend explaining the Popularity Contest to an acquaintance who needed a little lesson in proper etiquette. Sometimes they'll even let out a roar, giving the lion a good run for his money.

These experiences are most rewarding for me. When you coach someone about *your* experiences wearing the pants, you too will feel the same pride and sense of accomplishment by helping others.

Pant Secret

Sure, water is hot at 211 degrees. But with one extra degree what do you have? Boiling, scalding, sizzling hot water that has the *power to produce steam – that can energize machines to move mountains*. It's what keeps your train moving. Just one extra degree: *only a little bit more effort* to achieve exponential results.

I am going to ask you to add one final process to help you reach for every one of those 212 degrees...for without it, time will fade excitement, knowledge will erode and progress will be hindered. Last, but not least:

COMMITMENT

In order to succeed at wearing the pants, you must be completely committed to these principles and utilize them to promote personal growth. Wear your Pants of Respect every day and keep them clean and tidy. Like anything else that isn't maintained, your pants will become dirty, faded and wrinkled if not cared for.

Believe in yourself or no one will!

Always stay positive and *believe you will learn* to wear the pants.

A positive attitude means a healthier life. Researchers at the University of Texas and North Carolina State University have proven that people who maintain a positive attitude are significantly less likely to show signs of aging, and more likely to be stronger and healthier. If that's not reason enough to believe in yourself and maintain a positive attitude, what is?

Have faith in yourself and you'll achieve goals never thought possible. Self-respect is worth standing up for – as an equal, never tolerate being treated as an inferior. This commitment ensures you will coach others how to wear the pants.

Being committed gives you the fortitude to keep polishing this expertise. Soon, this practice becomes a habit – a habit you will protect. There will be many times in the future when you say, "That didn't work out so well!" Be committed to believing you did what you thought was right, eliminating feelings of self-doubt. Tell yourself, "Next time I will do it *this* way...."

Will it last?

We've all taken part in our share of motivational classes, listened to inspirational speeches and made one too many New Year's Resolutions. You're fired up. More inspired than ever before, you're ready to conquer the world! Sounds familiar, right? It's the same old story. Uplifting high-energy speeches and many resolutions leave you feeling excited, but within a few weeks, the memories fade and your resolution is over before it starts. There was no commitment to keep the inspiration alive.

Commitment is the steam to move mountains!

Yes, it will last – and here is why.

This time it is different. This time you've dug deeper past the surface of those motivational speeches and those empty promises. You have now studied the **Pant Principles** and understand the discipline involved in earning respect, and you will be ***reminded everyday*** of the need to wear the pants. The world is full of bullies, indifferent people, and snakes in the grass. You cannot avoid them and they *will be in your face*. When you feel ignored, used or abused, reassess your *commitment* to be *inspired* and *motivated* to stand up for yourself.

Pant Secret

Do not get mad at those dishing it out, as it is simply their nature. Rather, *get mad at yourself for allowing* it to continue to happen. It will secure your commitment to wearing the pants for the rest of your life.

"The definition of insanity is doing the same thing over and over again and expecting a different result."

~ Benjamin Franklin (1706 - 90) ~

This oft-quoted line reminds us of the simple truths of life. Too many times we sit by the wayside and let history repeat itself, even though we're unsatisfied with the outcome. So what are you going to do about it?

Pant Promise

During the next 24 hours I want you to show respect for two people in your life, beginning with the most important: YOURSELF. For once, forget the negatives you feel are wrong with your body, your knowledge, your expertise, and your past. Think about ONE thing you like about yourself and make this your focus. Respect yourself with the same reverence you have for royalty, celebrities, and those you respect the most.

Now decide on one person who *needs* your respect: maybe your spouse, a sibling, or an old friend. This may be someone for whom you've shown respect in the past, but for whatever reason you've stopped giving it. Just for 24 hours forgive their mistakes, overlook their shortcomings and treat them as you would a world leader. Shower them with honest praise and focus on their good qualities. Twenty-four hours is a short time to try - you CAN do this!

I hope you feel so good about giving respect that after this 24-hour test, you will set a 30-day goal to bestow everyone you encounter with genuine respect. By doing so, it will be *that much easier* to follow these Pant Principles for the rest of your life. And if you do, you have just accomplished your goal for having chosen to read this book in the first place.

To move a mountain start with a pebble and before long, it's gone!

Stay in control and enjoy the process of building, retaining and giving respect. History is there for you to write ... so what are you waiting for? Go live healthier, happier, and richer. Never stop short of that one final degree!

Let me know how it's going ... at

PantSecrets@aol.com

"The next edition may be about your Parables!"

Final Note: The pants on the cover of this book represent Pants of Respect, significant only to me and to those who have read this book. To wear them with pride, it takes confidence, self-respect, and a whole lot of practice. It's my goal to one day fill a stadium with a family of pant-wearers! I hope you are there!

Pant Check Finale

Congratulations – you have now solved the mystery and unlocked the secrets of respect. How do you feel about following the Pant Principles and Wearing The Pants?

	LOW				HIGH
Home:	**0**	**1**	**2**	**3**	**4**
Work:	**0**	**1**	**2**	**3**	**4**
Social Settings:	**0**	**1**	**2**	**3**	**4**

Today's Date: ______________________________

On the last day of the next three months, re-rate your progress in each category.

Date: ______________________________________

Date: ______________________________________

Date: ______________________________________

You should now be a bona fide member of my Pant-Wearing Family!

Order your *FREE (free means $0 cost, no shipping & handling) habit-breaker wrist band and bookmark reference guide at **www.WhoIsWearingThePants.com**,* ***or email PantSecrets@aol.com.***

NOTES:

Thanks and Praise

Every author has spent many hours, months or years putting thoughts onto paper. The process – from brainstorming through the revisions to publishing – is a journey all unto itself. Without support from others, this task would be most difficult or not doable at all.

To those who said, *"Dave, you should write that down,"* in response to my ideas, I thank you for letting me know you thought my words should be heard by others.

I also appreciate the honesty from those who said, *"David, I don't get it!"* This enticed me to re-think my position and fine-tune my thoughts to be clearer in meaning.

Several have urged me to just keep going. My good friend and published writer Richard Valentine urged me nearly every day to make a little progress. Being an avid reader, his quiet wisdom gave me direction to keep my words precise, without fluff, and was invaluable to my success.

My wife has told me for years to put my thoughts in a book. She always had an open ear (and good suggestions) when I would yell from my office, *"What's a better word for _____?"* Her continual support and thoughtful nudge of, "How is the book coming?" always encouraged me to invest an hour or two more each day to the keyboard.

A special thanks to my copy editor Laura Bliss Plekavic who was always there to ensure proper use of the language, with a superb ability to keep age and gender neutrality in place. Most important was her skill for offering a third party perspective of my thoughts when I would "hit the wall" and go blank.

To my high school English teacher, I'll bet you are quite surprised to see me, one of your least interested students in English class, write and publish a great book like this.

Unfortunately, the Acknowledgement page is the most unread section of a book and gratitude goes unnoticed. So, thanks to *YOU* for taking the time to read this page.

MEET THE AUTHOR –

David Hearld was born and raised in the small Midwestern farming and industrial town of Noblesville, Indiana. Seeking to broaden his horizons, David packed his bags for Muncie, Indiana, to pursue his degree at Ball State University.

His thirst for entrepreneurship started early in life with several moneymaking ventures in retail and wholesale management and ownership, leading to the creation of a nationwide distribution company servicing over 1,000 clients.

In 1991, David founded Gibraltar Group, Inc. (which he continues to oversee today), a consulting firm whose goal is to help individuals, families, and business owners to manage debt, increase income, and develop strategies for building better lives and businesses for the future.

Currently, David is the founder and CEO of Profit-Tell International, Inc. (http://www.Profit-Tell.com/), a marketing and advertising company with over 30 locations in North America. During the past 15 years his firm has placed over 13,600 marketing programs in a wide variety of business categories all over the world.

Beyond his business ventures, he was also a Mediator for the American Arbitration Association, President of National Floor Covering Association, Business and Marketing Consultant, Member of the National Franchise Association and Family Counselor. David has conducted hundreds of sales, motivational and marketing seminars in North America, Spain and Mexico, and is a nationally quoted expert on TheStreet.com, Sales & Marketing Management magazine, and Yahoo Financial! He is also learning to speak Chinese in his spare time.

Fueled by these endeavors, success stories and advice from other respected leaders over a period of 30 years, David has learned to develop methods for teaching individuals to improve their personal and business lives through positive behavior by earning respect – one of the greatest hallmarks of success and happiness.

David now lives with his wife in Hinsdale, Illinois, a suburb of Chicago, and has a grown daughter and son.